ENVIRONMENTAL NOISE POLLUTION

BOARD OF ADVISORS, ENGINEERING

ENVIRONMENTAL NOISE POLLUTION

PATRICK F. CUNNIFF
University of Maryland

John Wiley & Sons
New York Santa Barbara London
Sydney Toronto

Library of Congress Cataloging in Publication Data:

Cunniff, P F
  Environmental noise pollution.

  Includes index.
  1. Noise pollution.   I. Title.
TD892.C86   363.6   76-48146
ISBN 0-471-18943-X

Printed in the United States of America

10 9 8 7 6 5 4 3 2

PREFACE

Environmental noise pollution has been recognized in recent years as a serious threat to the quality of life enjoyed by the people in most industrialized nations. In 1969 the Walsh-Healey Public Contracts Act was amended to include for the first time a federal safety regulation on industrial noise exposure. These same allowable occupational noise levels were included in the Occupational Safety and Health Act of 1970 for industries engaged in interstate commerce. One year later, the U.S. Environmental Protection Agency submitted its "Report to the President and the Congress on Noise," which was an assessment of noise as a national pollution problem. Among the conclusions reached in the Report was a conservative estimate that at least 80 million people in the United States are exposed to noise levels that may have a significant impact on their health and welfare. This Report led to the passage of the Noise Control Act of 1972, which has far-reaching potential for controlling noise produced by major noise sources. State and local governments around the country have responded to the seriousness of the situation by enacting new legislation aimed at controlling the rising noise levels experienced by citizens in rural and urban areas.

I have developed a three-credit course on environmental noise pollution at the University of Maryland. This book is the product of the notes written for this course, which has been open to students with technical as well as nontechnical backgrounds. Consequently, the course content is developed in a way that each student may benefit from it especially from the first three chapters, which review basic laws of physics, some mathematics, and analysis techniques. This provides each student with a foundation in these fundamentals for the remainder of the text material on environmental noise pollution.

The experience of measuring the characteristics of sounds by special instruments is an important part of understanding how sound waves propagate. Chapter 4 introduces the common instrumentation used in measuring environmental noise pollution. After this introduction to measuring sounds, Chapter 5 considers some methods for controlling sounds generated indoors and outdoors.

Topics on speech, hearing, effects of noise on people, and special noise environments, such as the sonic boom, are covered in the next three chapters. Chapter 9 is devoted to outdoor community noise in which rating methods, such as the energy equivalent sound level and the day-night average level, are fully explained. Noise from transportation vehicles are examined in the next chapter, followed by a chapter on the special features of industrial noise. Finally, Chapter 12 reviews the development of noise control laws and ordinances at the federal, state, and local levels of government.

To assist the reader in comprehending the material, there is a summary of important ideas and equations at the end of each chapter, followed by assignments. These assignments include written responses to theory, definitions and terminology, mathematical problems and, when practical, suggested laboratory and field measurement exercises.

Few textbooks are written without the aide and assistance of others. In particular, I thank Dr. James Dally, former Chairman of the Mechanical Engineering Department, for his support in the development of the course on environmental noise pollution. I also extend my appreciation to my students, who provided helpful suggestions in the development of the course material. Finally, I thank my wife Patricia for the encouragement she gave me, and my children, Brian, John, Elizabeth, and Christopher, for the cooperation they gave me throughout the preparation of the manuscript.

Patrick F. Cunniff

CONTENTS

3

ANALYSIS OF SOUND WAVES 31

4

MEASURING SOUNDS 45

10

TRANSPORTATION NOISE 151

11

INDUSTRIAL NOISE 176

12

NOISE CONTROL LAWS AND ORDINANCES 190

A

SUMMARY OF NOISE RATING METHODS 201

ANSWERS TO EVEN-NUMBERED PROBLEMS 204

INDEX 207

1
BASIC CONCEPTS

We begin our examination of environmental noise pollution by introducing important physical laws and mathematical operations. This helps in forming a foundation to comprehend the technical material contained in this treatment of unwanted sound. In Chapter 1 we explain the ideas of units and dimensions used in mechanics, review some mathematical operations with logarithms, and examine what is meant by simple harmonic oscillation.

    At the end of each chapter there is a summary of the important ideas and equations contained in the chapter, followed by suggested assignments. These last two sections in each chapter should be helpful in evaluating your knowledge of the material.

1.1 Mechanics Review

In 1687 Sir Isaac Newton published his famous three laws for particle behavior. The second law, which is perhaps the most familiar of the three, can be written as:

$$\text{FORCE} = \text{MASS} \times \text{ACCELERATION} \tag{1.1}$$

This relationship is important, since the concepts of units and dimensions used in mechanics are based on this equation.

    When we measure the length of an object, we may record its length in meters, inches, or perhaps feet. The concept of length is called a *dimension*; the terms meters, inches, and feet are called *units*. The concept of time is also a dimension, for which the units may be seconds, minutes, hours, and the like. It has been agreed that length and time are fundamental to all systems in Newtonian mechanics and that either mass or force may be selected as the third fundamental dimension. A system in which mass, length, and time are

TABLE 1.1
Standard International Units and Abbreviations

Quantity	SI Unit	Abbreviations
Length	Meter	m
Time	Second	s
Mass	Kilogram	kg
Density	Kilogram per cubic meter	kg/m^3
Force	Newton	N
Velocity	Meter per second	m/s
Acceleration	Meter per square second	m/s^2
Pressure	Newton per square meter = Pascal	N/m^2 = Pa
Work	Newton-meter = joule	N-m = J
Power	Newton-meter per second = watt	N-m/s = W
Temperature	Degrees Kelvin	K

the fundamental dimensions is called an *absolute system*. If the dimension of force is selected instead of the mass, we then have a *gravitational system* composed of force, length, and time as the fundamental dimensions.

We shall use the standard international system (SI), which is an absolute system. The units in this system include the following: length is in meters (m), mass is in kilograms (kg), time is in seconds (s), and force is in newtons (N). From Newton's second law, a mass of 1 kg experiences an acceleration of 1 m/s^2 under the influence of a force of 1 N. Referring to Equation 1.1,

$$1 \text{ N} = 1 \text{ kg} \times 1 \text{ m/s}^2$$

Table 1.1 lists some important quantities that we shall use in our study of environmental noise pollution, while Table 1.2 shows useful conversions from the English gravitational system to the SI system. There will be situations when we shall deviate from the SI system in favor of English system, such as when we quote an existing noise ordinance that may require noise

TABLE 1.2
**Conversions Between the English System and
the Standard International System**

To Convert from	To	Multiply by
Feet	Meters	0.3048
Pounds (force)	Newtons	4.448
Pound-feet	Joules	1.356
Pounds per square inch	Pascals	6,895
Pounds per square foot	Pascals	47.88
Horsepower	Watts	745.7
Miles per hour	Kilometers per hour	1.609

level measurements at 50 ft. In these cases, the equivalent SI unit will follow in parentheses, such as 50 ft (15.3 m).

Some important quantities from Table 1.1 are explained below.

WEIGHT. The gravitational force of attraction exerted on a body by the earth is called the weight of the body. It can be shown from Newton's law of gravitation that the acceleration of gravity, g, on the earth's surface is:

$$g = 9.81 \text{ m/s}^2$$

This means that if you drop an object close to the earth's surface, it moves toward the ground at this acceleration. Therefore the weight is related to the mass by Equation 1.1 as:

$$\text{WEIGHT} = \text{MASS} \times g \tag{1.2}$$

PRESSURE. Pressure represents the distribution of a force over an area. In mathematical form,

$$\text{PRESSURE} = \frac{\text{FORCE}}{\text{AREA}} \tag{1.3}$$

The units for pressure are newtons per square meter, or the Pascal, where $1 \text{ Pa} = 1 \text{ N/m}^2$. As an example, if the gas inside the cylinder in Figure 1.1 exerts a net pressure of 20 Pa on a piston of area 2 m², then the force equals 40 N. Another example of pressure is the atmospheric pressure given in the daily weather forecasts. At standard atmospheric conditions, it is interesting to note that the atmospheric pressure is approximately 101,300 Pa.

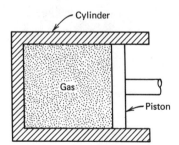

FIGURE 1.1   A gas in a cylinder exerting pressure on a piston.

DENSITY. The mass per unit volume is called the density. We know that a cube of lead is heavier or more dense than a cube of wood. In environmental noise pollution we shall be referring to the density of air, which at atmospheric pressure and room temperature equals 1.18 kg/m³.

WORK. Energy can usually be converted to useful work, where by work we mean the following.

$$\text{WORK} = \text{FORCE} \times \text{DISTANCE} \tag{1.4}$$

The units for work are newton-meter, or the joule, where 1 N-m = 1 J. For example, if the piston in Figure 1.1 moves through a distance of 0.1 m under a constant force of 40 N, then the work done by the gas acting on the piston equals 4 N-m = 4 J.

POWER. Power is defined as the time rate of doing work. Thus,

$$\text{POWER} = \frac{\text{WORK}}{\text{TIME}} \tag{1.5}$$

The units for power are newton-meters per second, which is equivalent to the more familiar unit, the watt. If the above work of 4 N-m occurs during a 0.01-s interval, then the power associated with this interval is 400 N-m/s = 400 W. The power developed by machines is frequently rated in horsepower, which can be converted to watts, as shown in Table 1.2. However, in acoustics we always express the sound power radiated by a sound source in watts.

Note that henceforth units will normally be abbreviated as provided in Table 1.1 where convenient.

1.2 Mathematics Review

The following is a review of mathematics generally required for routine calculations in environmental noise pollution.

(a) **EXPONENT REPRESENTATION.** When we have large or small numbers, we express the number in exponent form for convenience. Consider the following examples.

$$\begin{aligned}
1,000,000 &= 10^6 & 10 &= 10^1 \\
100,000 &= 10^5 & 1 &= 10^0 \\
10,000 &= 10^4 & 0.1 &= 10^{-1} \\
1,000 &= 10^3 & 0.01 &= 10^{-2} \\
100 &= 10^2 & 0.001 &= 10^{-3}
\end{aligned}$$

Other examples include: $0.00002 = 20 \times 10^{-6}$; $29,600,000 = 29.6 \times 10^6$.

(b) **LOGARITHMS.** By definition, if $a^b = c$, then the logarithm of c to the base a equals b. Mathematically, this is expressed as:

$$\log_a c = b \tag{1.6}$$

For our purposes, we shall be using the number 10 as the base b, so that logarithms are written as:

$$\log_{10} c = \log c$$

where we have dropped the base 10 for convenience.

From the definition of the logarithm to the base 10, we observe the following from the above exponent representation of numbers.

$\log 1000 = 3.0$	$\log 0.1 = -1.0 = 9.0 - 10$
$\log 100 = 2.0$	$\log 0.01 = -2.0 = 8.0 - 10$
$\log 10 = 1.0$	$\log 0.001 = -3.0 = 7.0 - 10$
$\log 1 = 0$	$\log 0.0001 = -4.0 = 6.0 - 10$

We see from the above that the logarithm of a number between 100 and 1000 must be between 2.0 and 3.0. In fact,

$$\log 400 = 2.602$$

Here, the digit 2 is called the characteristic and .602 is called the mantissa, which we obtain from a table of logarithms or a slide rule. Of course, with the advent of the small electronic calculator, the result is immediately obtained by pressing a few buttons.

In the case of a number less than unity, the logarithm is a negative quantity. For example, to obtain the logarithm of 0.004, we see from the above that it must lie between -2.0 and -3.0. To arrive at the solution, we use the alternate form of $7.0 - 10$, since the tables of logarithms are listed only for positive numbers. Thus,

$$\log 0.004 = 7.602 - 10 = -2.398$$

Here the characteristic is $7.0 - 10$, while the mantissa is .602.

Example 1.1
Find the logarithm of the following numbers: (a) 2, (b) 50, (c) 0.0065, and (d) 0.091.

(a) $\log 2 = 0.301$
(b) $\log 50 = 1.699$
(c) $\log 0.0065 = 7.813 - 10 = -2.187$
(d) $\log 0.091 = 8.959 - 10 = -1.041$

(c) **ALGEBRAIC LAWS.** The following are three useful algebraic laws associated with logarithms.

$$\log ab = \log a + \log b$$

$$\log \frac{a}{b} = \log a - \log b$$

$$\log a^n = n \log a$$

Example 1.2

If $z = rs/t$, find $\log z$.

$$\log z = \log\left(\frac{rs}{t}\right) = \log(rs) - \log t$$
$$= \log r + \log s - \log t \qquad \text{Answer}$$

Example 1.3

If $x = (5320)^{3.2}$, find $\log x$.

One approach is to use the algebraic laws as follows.

$$\log x = \log(5320)^{3.2} = 3.2 \log(5320) = 3.2 \log(5.32 \times 1000)$$
$$= 3.2(\log 5.32 + \log 1000) = 3.2(0.726 + 3) = 11.92 \qquad \text{Answer}$$

Example 1.4

Find $\log 0.00065$.

The algebraic laws and the exponent representation may be used as follows.

$$\log 0.00065 = \log(6.5 \times 10^{-4}) = \log 6.5 + \log 10^{-4}$$
$$= 0.813 - 4 \log 10 = 0.813 - 4$$
$$= -3.187 \qquad \text{Answer}$$

(d) **ANTILOGARITHMS.** The inverse of the logarithm is called the antilogarithm. For instance, since

$$\log 3.2 = 0.505$$

then

$$\text{antilog } 0.505 = 3.2$$

As another example, consider the following.

$$\log(2 \times 10^8) = \log 2 + 8 \log 10 = 0.301 + 8.0 = 8.301$$

Therefore,

$$\text{antilog } 8.301 = 2.0 \times 10^8$$

Note that in calculating the antilogarithm of a number, the digit before the decimal point is the characteristic and the digits to the right of the decimal point represent the mantissa. We look up the antilog of the mantissa, place a decimal point after the first digit from the logarithmic table, and multiply the result by 10 to the power of the characteristic. Further examples include

$$\text{antilog } 2.65 = 4.47 \times 10^2$$
$$\text{antilog } 6.65 = 4.47 \times 10^6$$

To find the antilog of a negative quantity, first note that

$$\log 0.091 = 8.959 - 10 = -1.041$$

Thus,

$$\text{antilog}\,(-1.041) = \text{antilog}\,(8.959 - 10) = 9.10 \times 10^{-2} = 0.091$$

Here we arrange the negative number in the form of a negative characteristic and a positive mantissa. Looking up the antilog of the mantissa, we place a decimal point after the first digit from the table and multiply by 10 to the power of the characteristic. Further examples include

$$\text{antilog}\,(-2.345) = \text{antilog}\,(7.655 - 10) = 4.52 \times 10^{-3}$$
$$\text{antilog}\,(-4.910) = \text{antilog}\,(5.090 - 10) = 1.23 \times 10^{-5}$$

Example 1.5
If $L = 10 \log B$, find B if (a) $L = 45$, (b) $L = 70$, and (c) $L = 98$.
    (a) Since $L = 10 \log B$
        then $B = \text{antilog}\,(L/10)$
               $B = \text{antilog}\,4.5 = 3.16 \times 10^{4}$
    (b) $B = \text{antilog}\,7.0 = 1.0 \times 10^{7}$
    (c) $B = \text{antilog}\,9.8 = 6.31 \times 10^{9}$

1.3 Simple Harmonic Oscillation

As an introduction to understanding the behavior of sound waves, we begin by explaining what is meant by simple harmonic oscillation. Consider the motion of the pendulum of a clock shown in Figure 1.2. The pendulum motion is described by the angle θ measured off the fixed verticle line. Let θ_o be the initial displacement of the pendulum when it is relased from rest.

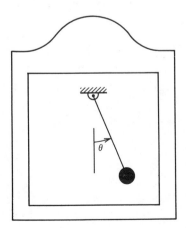

FIGURE 1.2 The pendulum of a clock demonstrating simple harmonic oscillation.

The pendulum travels from one side to the other and returns to where it started, only to repeat the cycle again. If it takes 1 s to complete a cycle, its frequency of oscillation equals 1 cps. However, if it takes only 1/2 s to complete a cycle, the frequency equals 2 cps. Currently, the term Hertz (Hz) is used to describe frequency, where 1 Hz equals 1 cps.

The actual motion of the pendulum released from rest for small displacements about the fixed vertical line is described by the following relationship.

$$\theta = \theta_o \cos 2\pi f t \tag{1.7}$$

in which θ_o = initial angular displacement in radians
$\quad\quad f$ = frequency of the pendulum motion in Hertz
$\quad\quad t$ = time in seconds

and cos is the abbreviation of the trigonometric cosine function. The argument $(2\pi f t)$ of the cosine is in radians, where there are 2π rad in $360°$. Note that the circular frequency $\omega = 2\pi f$ in radians per second is sometimes used for convenience. Equation 1.7 is plotted in Figure 1.3 in which the time t is plotted along the abscissa axis (horizontal axis) and the angular displacement θ is plotted along the ordinate axis (vertical axis). The time it takes to complete one cycle is labeled as the period, T, in the figure, while the peak amplitude is labeled θ_o. We note that the period of oscillation and the frequency are related by

$$T = \frac{1}{f} \tag{1.8}$$

For example, if the frequency equals 4 Hz, the corresponding period equals 0.25 s.

In environmental noise pollution we are concerned with this type of behavior, which is called simple harmonic oscillation. It can be shown that the trigonometric sine function, abbreviated as sin, and the cosine function describe harmonic oscillations mathematically. We shall have occasion to refer to these functions when we examine the combination of pure tones in Chapter 2.

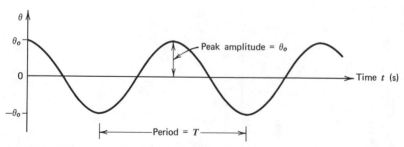

FIGURE 1.3 The angular displacement-time history for the simple harmonic oscillation of the pendulum.

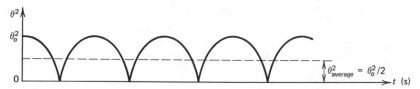

FIGURE 1.4　The square of the angular displacement-time history for the simple harmonic oscillation of the pendulum.

Usually we wish to know something about the average amplitude of the oscillation. From Figure 1.3 it is clear that the average of θ over a period is zero. Consequently, we first square the function as shown in Figure 1.4 and then calculate the average of the square values. Having this numerical value, we then calculate its square root to obtain what is called the root-mean-square (rms) value. It can be shown that for simple harmonic oscillation, $\theta_{avg}^2 = \theta_o^2/2$, so that the root-mean-square value equals

$$\theta_{rms} = \frac{\theta_o}{\sqrt{2}} = 0.707\theta_o \tag{1.9}$$

As a second example of simple harmonic oscillation, consider a mechanical oscillator consisting of a mass supported on rollers and connected by an elastic spring to a moving surface as shown in Figure 1.5. Assume that a steady supply of energy exists that causes the surface to oscillate in simple harmonic motion. The vibrating surface will impart motion to the mass through the elastic spring. If the vibrating surface moves with simple harmonic oscillation at some frequency f, then the mass also experiences simple harmonic oscillation at the same frequency.

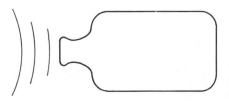

FIGURE 1.5　A mechanical oscillator connected to a moving surface undergoing simple harmonic oscillation.

The acoustic analogy of the mechanical oscillator is called a Helmholtz resonator, which looks like the jug shown in Figure 1.6. Here pressure oscillations outside the resonator provide the steady energy source so that

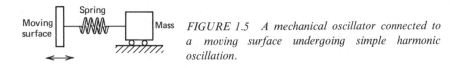

FIGURE 1.6　A Helmholtz oscillator excited by external sound pressure oscillations.

the air inside experiences simple harmonic oscillations like the mechanical oscillator. It is interesting to realize that both the mechanical oscillator and the Helmholtz resonator are sometimes used as external attachments to bodies so as to suppress mechanical oscillations and noise, respectively, in a narrow frequency range.

Suppose we add additional springs and masses to our original mass-spring model as shown in Figure 1.7. Now the motion of the moving surface produces motion of all three masses. That is, there is a continuous transfer of energy through the elastic medium represented by the chain of springs and masses. This phenomenon represents a propagation of energy through the elastic medium. We shall find this concept of energy propagation helpful in understanding sound wave propagation as developed in Chapter 2.

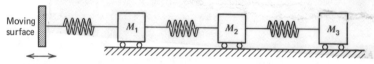

FIGURE 1.7   *A chain of masses and springs connected to a moving surface undergoing simple harmonic oscillation.*

1.4 Summary
A. The important ideas:
1. We use the standard international system for the units in environmental noise pollution.
2. Logarithms will be to the base 10.
3. Simple harmonic oscillation may be described by either $\sin(2\pi ft)$ or $\cos(2\pi ft)$.
4. The root-mean-square value is an important measurement of a quantity experiencing harmonic oscillations.

B. The important equations:

1. FORCE = MASS × ACCELERATION   (1.1)

2. $\theta = \theta_o \cos 2\pi ft$ (1.7)

3. $T = \dfrac{1}{f}$ (1.8)

4. $\theta_{rms} = \dfrac{\theta_o}{\sqrt{2}}$ (1.9)

1.5 Assignments
1.1   What units are assigned to the dimensions of mass, length, time, and force in the SI system?

1.2 If a body weighs 98.1 N on the earth's surface, calculate its mass in kilograms.

1.3 (a) Calculate your weight in newtons. (b) Convert 35 mi/h to km/h.

1.4 (a) How long is a football field in meters? (b) Calculate your height in meters.

1.5 The pressure exerted over a rectangular plate 2 m long and 3 m wide is 2.4×10^{-3} Pa. What is the corresponding force?

1.6 A machine is rated to deliver 100 hp. Express this power in watts.

1.7 A sphere of radius 0.1 m weighs 100 N. Calculate its density. (*Hint.* The volume of a sphere $= 4\pi r^3/3$.)

1.8 Explain the difference between the weight of an object and its mass.

1.9 Express each of the following numbers by the exponent representation such that there is one digit before the decimal point: (a) 16,400, (b) -0.024, (c) 3,000,000, (d) 0.0000008.

1.10 Find the logarithms for: (a) 200, (b) 86.3, (c) 1455, (d) 0.44.

1.11 Find the logarithms for: (a) 7.96, (b) 0.02, (c) 0.00032, (d) 0.16.

1.12 Find log A if A equals (a) $(322)^{-2.6}$, (b) $(6.2)^8$.

1.13 Find log A if A equals (a) $(0.0045)^{3.6}$, (b) $(0.9)^{-1.4}$.

1.14 Find the antilogs for: (a) 12, (b) 0.0122.

1.15 Find the antilogs for: (a) 2.4, (b) 0.00089

1.16 Find the antilogs for: (a) -1.36, (b) -0.75

1.17 Find the antilogs for: (a) -3.0, (b) -0.094

1.18 Evaluate: (a) $10^{3.41}$, (b) $10^{8.25}$.

1.19 Find $L = 10 \log (I/I_0)$, if $I = 9.5 \times 10^{-3}$ and $I_0 = 10^{-12}$.

1.20 If the measured period for simple harmonic motion is 0.04 s, what is the frequency in Hertz? What is the circular frequency ω in radians per second?

1.21 If a body experiences simple harmonic motion with a peak amplitude of 4.243×10^{-3} m, what is the corresponding root-mean-square amplitude?

1.22 Plot two cycles of $X = 20 \cos 2\pi ft$ using the abscissa axis in units of $2\pi ft$ (radians) for (a) $f = 100$ Hz, and (b) $f = 200$ Hz.

2
BEHAVIOR OF SOUND WAVES

Wave propagation phenomena can be readily observed. For example, a stone dropped into a pond causes ripples of waves to propagate radially outward on its surface. If a rope is snapped at one end, we observe a wave traveling down the rope to the opposite end. Sound wave propagation, however, is one that we cannot see but can hear because of the pressure oscillations our ears are capable of detecting. For example, we observe that there is a short interval between the initial flash of a fireworks display and the booming sound we hear later. That is, it takes time for the sound to travel or propagate through the air before it reaches us.

The relationships for finding the speed of sound wave motion are reviewed in this chapter along with some important equations relating sound intensity, sound power, and sound pressure. We shall also develop some ways in which sound wave paths are obstructed because of reflection, diffraction, and refraction. The summation of sound waves is examined to find the resulting root-mean-square (rms) pressure, a result that is most important in acoustics. Finally, the idea of spectrum analysis of sound waves (i.e., relating sound pressure amplitude with frequency) is developed using examples taken from musical notes and everyday sounds.

2.1 Sound Wave Propagation

Sound waves are elastic waves that may be produced by vibrating bodies or air turbulence. The sound waves propagate through media such as air, which possesses mass and elasticity. The air molecules oscillate back and forth about their equilibrium position, somewhat like the masses in Figure 1.7. The molecules closest to the vibrating body are compressed initially. This compression causes adjacent molecules to move. The motion of successive molecules continues as the sound waves travel through the medium. Each

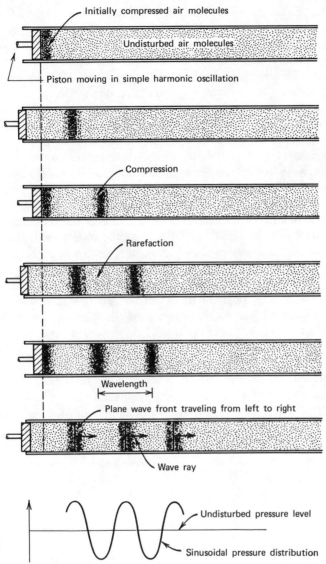

Initially compressed air molecules

Undisturbed air molecules

Piston moving in simple harmonic oscillation

Compression

Rarefaction

Wavelength

Plane wave front traveling from left to right

Wave ray

Undisturbed pressure level

Sinusoidal pressure distribution

FIGURE 2.1   Plane sound wave propagation in a tube generated by a piston moving in simple harmonic oscillation.

molecule moves back and forth about its original undisturbed (equilibrium) position as it undergoes periodic compression (increase in pressure) and rarefaction (decrease in pressure).

Figure 2.1 shows a series of sketches of sound wave propagation in a tube generated by a piston at the left end moving in simple harmonic oscillation. When the piston moves to the right, the air molecules closest to the piston experience a pressure increase; when the piston moves to the left, these molecules experience a pressure decrease. Because of the elasticity of the medium, adjacent air molecules will also experience similar changes in pressure after a short time has elapsed. The distance between the pressure peaks measures the wavelength, as shown in Figure 2.1. The wavelength is related to the period of the generated sound in that it takes one period for the wave front to travel one wavelength. We also note that the pressure change relative to the undisturbed pressure varies sinusoidally. The waves move in parallel planes in this example. Such waves are called plane waves. The planes of maximum compression are labeled as the wave front and the direction of the traveling wave front is labeled as the wave ray, as shown in Figure 2.1.

As a second example of sound wave propagation, consider the pulsating balloon in Figure 2.2. As the spherical surface of the balloon oscillates radially, a series of adjacent molecular spheres will be set into oscillation at the same frequency as the pulsating balloon. As the sound wave reaches a particular set of molecules, the molecules are compressed so that the pressure increases above the atmospheric pressure. Following the compression of the molecules, there is a reduction of air pressure and rarefaction occurs. The waves developed by this physical model are called spherical waves. We observe from Figure 2.2 that the wave rays from the spherical waves are no longer parallel to each other as in the case of plane wave propagation. Such waves are assumed to emanate from sound sources, provided that the dimensions of the source are small relative to the wavelength generated. We call sound sources that generate spherical waves point sources.

Other examples of vibrating sound sources include the vocal chords in our larynx when we talk or sing, vibrating air columns in wind instruments such as the clarinet, vibrating membranes of drums, and vibrating strings of a violin. Air turbulence from wind around microphones is also a source of sound that is sometimes troublesome when making outdoor sound pressure measurements.

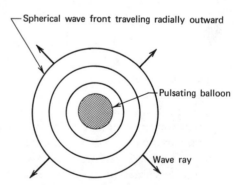

Spherical wave front traveling radially outward

Pulsating balloon

Wave ray

FIGURE 2.2   Spherical sound wave propagation generated by a pulsating balloon.

2.2 Speed of Propagation

From physics it is shown that the speed of propagation of elastic waves is related to the two properties of the medium: the elasticity and the density. The speed at which a sound wave travels through a solid or liquid medium is given by the following relationship.

$$c = \sqrt{\frac{E}{\rho}} \tag{2.1}$$

in which c = speed of propagation in meters per second
E = Young's elastic modulus in newtons per square meter
ρ = density of the medium in kilograms per cubic meter

In the case of sound waves traveling through air in which the air is assumed to behave as an ideal gas, it can be shown that the speed of propagation is related to the air temperature as follows.

$$c = 20\sqrt{K} \tag{2.2}$$

in which K is the air temperature in degrees Kelvin. The temperature in degrees Kelvin and degrees Celsius, C, is related by

$$K = C + 273 \tag{2.3}$$

The speed of propagation through air at room temperature (22°C) is 344 m/s. Using Equation 2.1, it can be shown that the speed of propagation through water is 1410 m/s; through steel it is 5000 m/s; and through lead it is 1200 m/s. This means that sounds are capable of traveling at different speeds through all kinds of media, except a vacuum. The actual speed depends not only on the elastic modulus or stiffness of the medium, but also the medium density.

The distance traveled Δs by a body moving at a uniform speed v, during a time interval Δt, is given by the product of the speed and the time interval.

$$\Delta s = v(\Delta t) \tag{2.4}$$

In the case of a sound wave traveling at the speed of propagation, c, the period T represents the time it takes for the wave to travel the distance represented by the wavelength λ. Substituting for this into Equation 2.4, we obtain.

$$\lambda = cT \tag{2.5}$$

Since the period T equals the reciprocal of the frequency f, this equation is rewritten as

$$c = \lambda f \tag{2.6}$$

in which c = speed of propagation in meters per second
λ = wavelength in meters
f = frequency in Hertz

We conclude from the above relationships that the speed of propagation of an elastic wave is related to the elasticity and density of the medium through which the wave travels. If the medium is air, assumed to behave as an ideal gas, then we need only the temperature of the air to establish the propagation speed. Also, from Equation 2.6, we observe that once the speed of propagation is established for the medium, we can calculate the wavelength knowing the frequency of the sound source.

Example 2.1

A body oscillates in simple harmonic motion at 500 Hz. If the air temperature is 10°C, find the wavelength of the sound wave generated by the vibrating body.

Since the temperature is in degrees Celsius, first convert to the Kelvin scale. Referring to Equation 2.3,

$$K = C + 273$$
$$= 10 + 273 = 283°K$$

From Equation 2.2,

$$c = 20\sqrt{283} = 336 \frac{m}{s}$$

Rearranging Equation 2.6,

$$\lambda = \frac{c}{f} = \frac{336}{500} = 0.672 \text{ m} \qquad \text{Answer}$$

2.3 Sound Intensity and Sound Power

In sound wave propagation the vibrating body transmits energy through the elastic medium, causing the molecules in the medium to be set into oscillation. The energy-flow through the medium per unit area per unit of time is defined as the *sound intensity*, I. The units for sound intensity are watts/ per square meter. Since energy per unit time (or work per unit time) equals the sound power W, we relate the intensity and power as:

$$\text{INTENSITY} = \frac{\text{POWER}}{\text{AREA}} \qquad (2.7)$$

Note that both the intensity and power are root-mean-square quantities. For the case of a point source, we assume that a spherical wave is propagated. At a distance r from the point source, the surface area of the spherical wave front equals $4\pi r^2$, so that the sound intensity at this distance from the source is

$$I = \frac{W}{4\pi r^2} \qquad (2.8)$$

We observe that the intensity decreases inversely as the square of the distance from the sound source, which generates a fixed amount of sound power. This effect is called the "inverse square law" for the sound intensity.

Another important relationship in environmental noise pollution involves the sound intensity with the root-mean-square pressure experienced by the air molecules as the sound wave propagates through the medium; that is,

$$I = \frac{p^2}{\rho c} \qquad (2.9)$$

in which p = root-mean-square sound pressure in Pascals
$\quad\quad \rho$ = air density in kilograms per cubic meter
$\quad\quad c$ = speed of propagation in meters per second
$\quad\quad \rho c$ = specific acoustic impedance of the medium in kilograms per square meter-second

Equation 2.9 is true for both plane waves and spherical waves. If we have a means of measuring the root-mean-square pressure, then the sound intensity is known from Equation 2.9. Having the sound intensity, the distance from the source, and assuming freely propagating spherical waves from the source, we can calculate the sound power from Equation 2.8. This is the basis of one procedure used in establishing the sound power of industrial products.

Example 2.2

If the sound power from a small source equals 40 W, what is the intensity at (a) 10 m and (b) at 20 m from the source?

Assuming spherical waves, $I = W/4\pi r^2$. Thus,

(a) $I = 40/4\pi(10)^2 = 3.18 \times 10^{-2} \text{W/m}^2$ $\quad$ Answer
(b) $I = 40/4\pi(20)^2 = 0.796 \times 10^{-2} \text{W/m}^2$ $\quad$ Answer

Example 2.3

Find the root-mean-square pressure of a spherical wave whose intensity equals 2 W/m² at room temperature.

Rearranging Equation 2.9,

$$p^2 = I\rho c$$

At room temperature, $t = 22°C$. Therefore,

$$K = C + 273 = 295°K$$

$$c = 20\sqrt{295} = 344 \frac{m}{s}$$

Recalling that the density of air at standard atmospheric conditions is 1.18 kg/m³, we can substitute into the pressure-intensity equation as follows.

$$p^2 = 2\frac{W}{m^2} \times 1.18 \frac{kg}{m^3} \times 344 \frac{m}{s} = 812 \frac{W - kg}{m^4 - s}$$

Recall that 1 W = 1 N-m/s and 1 kg = 1 N-s^2/m. Thus,

$$p^2 = 812 \frac{\text{N-m}}{\text{s}} \times \frac{\text{N-s}^2}{\text{m}} \times \frac{1}{\text{m}^4 - \text{s}} = 812 \frac{\text{N}^2}{\text{m}^4}$$

$$p = 28.5 \frac{\text{N}}{\text{m}^2} = 28.5 \text{ Pa} \qquad \text{Answer}$$

In this example all the units were deliberately included to assure ourselves that the units balanced out to give us the correct units for the pressure.

2.4 Reflection of Sound Waves

It was assumed that the plane waves generated by the moving piston in Figure 2.1 and the spherical waves generated by the pulsating balloon in Figure 2.2 were unobstructed as they propagated through the air. Such waves are called *free progressive waves*. Generally, however, waves impinge on surfaces so that their paths are altered.

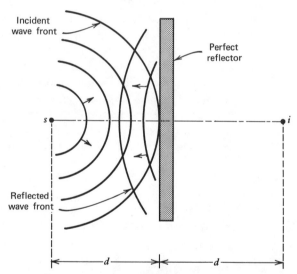

FIGURE 2.3 Sound waves from a point source s reflected by a perfect reflector.

As an example, consider a wall as a perfect reflector (no sound transmitted through the wall), as shown in Figure 2.3. When the incident spherical waves (i.e., the waves generated by the point source s) impinge on the wall, reflected waves occur. The reflected wave fronts are constructed by means of a compass using an imaginary source labeled i on the opposite side of the wall, at an equal distance d to the wall as the source. Because the pressures associated with the incident waves and the reflected waves are additive, it is important to remember that attempts to measure the sound intensity of the incident wave near reflecting surfaces can give misleading results.

The laws of reflection apply to sound waves impinging on a solid barrier at an angle, as shown in Figure 2.4. Both the source s and imaginary source i are shown in the figure. Here the direction of the sound wave fronts are labeled as wave rays. The angle of incidence θ_i and the angle of reflection θ_r are measured, as shown in Figure 2.4, between the wave rays and a line perpendicular to the barrier, respectively. The laws of reflection for sound waves are as follows.

1. The angle of incidence θ_i equals the angle of reflection θ_r.
2. The incident propagation, the reflected propagation, and the perpendicular line all lie in the same plane.

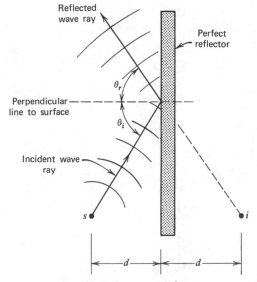

FIGURE 2.4   Example of the laws of reflection for sound waves from a point source s.

Standing waves are an interesting example of reflected sound waves that can occur in enclosed spaces with parallel surfaces Here the waves are reflected off the parallel walls in such a way that there are positions in the room where the pressure amplitudes from incident waves and the pressure amplitudes from the reflected waves reinforce each other and other positions where they cancel each other. Such a situation should be avoided for a room to have good acoustic properties. This may be achieved by altering the room geometry as well as the sound absorption characteristics of the room.

2.5 **Diffraction of Sound Waves**

Sound waves bend around edges of walls and pass through openings in windows. This ability to pass around or through an obstacle is called diffraction. The degree of diffraction depends on the wavelength of the sound wave and the dimensions of the obstacle. The larger the wavelength relative to the dimensions of the obstacle, the greater the diffraction. Figures 2.5 and 2.6 demonstrate this point. Figure 2.5 shows two cases of plane waves meeting an opening in a perfect reflecting wall. In Figure 2.5a the opening is small compared to the wavelength. Here the diffracted waves develop as though there were a point source in the opening of reduced sound energy, since most of the energy is contained in the reflected waves. However, Figure 2.5b shows

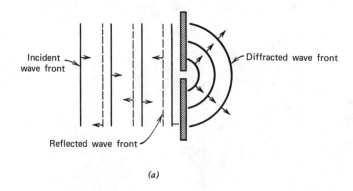

(a)

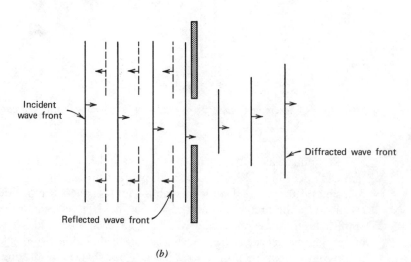

(b)

FIGURE 2.5   Examples of diffraction of plane sound waves through openings.

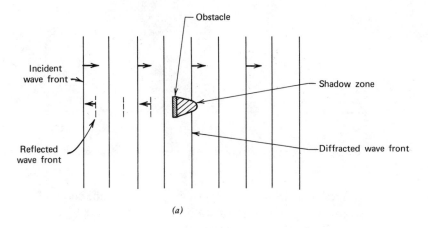

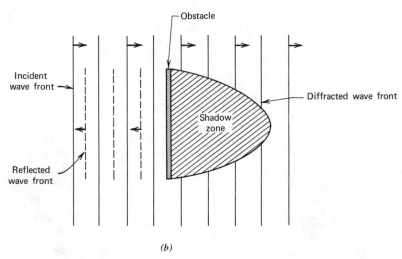

FIGURE 2.6 *Examples of diffraction of plane sound waves around obstacles.*

a large opening in which the diffracted waves are transmitted with no loss in their sound intensity. Figures 2.6a and 2.6b show the cases of diffraction of plane sound waves meeting both a small and a large obstacle, respectively. Both sketches show shadow zones developed behind each obstacle. These shadow zones are related to the size of the object for the same size wavelength and represent regions where the sound waves do not propagate.

2.6 Refraction of Sound Waves

Sound wave fronts may be distorted due to temperature changes throughout the medium. For example, if the temperature is warm on the earth's surface

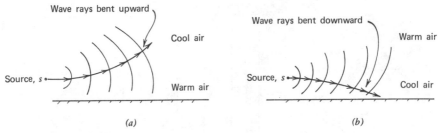

FIGURE 2.7   *Refraction of sound waves caused by outdoor temperature variations.*

and decreases with elevation as shown in Figure 2.7*a*, the speed of propagation is no longer constant along a given wave front. Consequently, the region of the wave front close to the earth's surface moves faster than the region of the same wave front at higher elevations. This bending phenomena of sound waves is called refraction. Figure 2.7*b* shows refraction for the case where the temperature increases with elevation so that the wave front is bent downward. It is important to realize that refraction can have a significant bearing on outdoor measurements, particularly in the case of distant sound sources, since the pressure levels may be reinforced or diminished due to a sharp temperature range of the air with elevation.

Wind gradients can also cause refraction. Since the windspeed normally increases with the height above the ground, the sound rays upwind from a source will be bent upward, producing a shadow zone close to the ground. Downwind there will be no shadow zone on the earth's surface, since the sound rays are bent downward.

2.7 Absorption and Transmission of Sound Waves

When an incident sound wave strikes a nonrigid barrier, in addition to the reflected waves, there is a transmitted wave through the barrier of reduced energy. This reduction in energy occurs because a portion of the incident sound energy excites the fibers on the barrier's surface into oscillation. This oscillatory energy in turn is converted to thermal energy because of the material's frictional behavior. This mechanism of energy reduction is fostered by materials containing porous openings, slits, and so forth, which produce a twisting path of the sound wave in the medium. Draperies, acoustic tile, and heavy room furnishings are particularly effective in absorbing sound energy in this manner.

The general case of plane sound rays traveling through three different media is shown in Figure 2.8. Assuming a steady sound source is in medium I, the incident ray travels from left to right in our figure. A reflected ray and a transmitted ray into medium II develop at the boundary between media I and II. The transmitted wave into medium II develops a reflected wave back

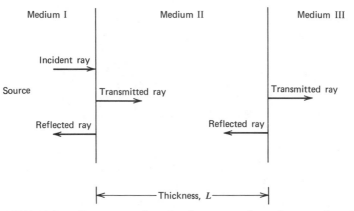

FIGURE 2.8   Successive reflected and transmitted sound rays in three different media.

into medium II and a transmitted wave into medium III at the boundary between these two media. This process of reflection and transmission at the boundaries continues indefinitely for the successive rays from the steady sound source. The steady-state sound intensity of the rays that are reflected back into medium I and those that are transmitted into medium III depend on the medium density, the speed of propagation of each medium, and the thickness L of medium II.

The practical applications of these results are important in noise control techniques. For example, suppose medium II represented a wall that is to be designed so as to restrict the amount of sound intensity entering a room adjacent to a noise source. Assuming that media I and III are air in this case, one could select a material of a certain thickness that would transmit the sounds into the receiving room at the prescribed level. We shall have more to say about this noise control technique in Chapter 5.

2.8 Summation of Pure Tones

Let the pressure variation at a fixed location from a pure tone generator be represented by the sine wave, as shown in Figure 2.9a. The mathematical expression is:

$$p_1 = P_1 \sin(\omega_1 t + \phi_1) \tag{2.10}$$

in which P_1 = peak pressure amplitude
ω_1 = circular frequency
t = time
ϕ_1 = phase angle

Add this expression to another sine wave shown in Figure 2.9b, which has different values of peak amplitude pressure, frequency, and phase angle. The

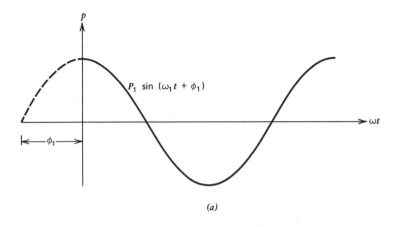

(a)

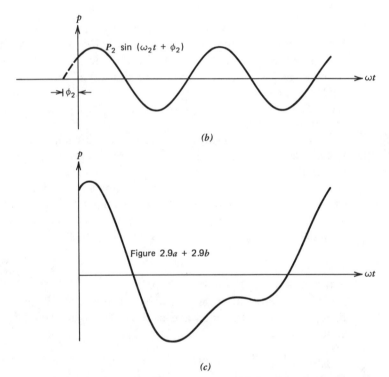

(b)

(c)

FIGURE 2.9   Example of two pure tones added to form a complex wave.

resulting pressure from the two waves is

$$p = P_1 \sin(\omega_1 t + \phi_1) + P_2 \sin(\omega_2 t + \phi_2) \tag{2.11}$$

The resulting complex wave is shown in Figure 2.9c. Having added the two expressions, now square both sides of Equation 2.11, and then take the time average of the result. It can be shown that the following expression is obtained, provided $\omega_1 \neq \omega_2$.

$$(p)^2_{avg} = \left(\frac{P_1}{\sqrt{2}}\right)^2 + \left(\frac{P_2}{\sqrt{2}}\right)^2 \tag{2.12}$$

Since the terms $(P_1/\sqrt{2})^2$ and $(P_2/\sqrt{2})^2$ are the mean-square values of their respective pressure waves in Figures 2.9a and 2.9b, we can rewrite Equation 2.12 as

$$(p)^2_{avg} = (p_1)^2_{avg} + (p_2)^2_{avg} \tag{2.13}$$

Taking the square root of both sides of Equation 2.13,

$$p_{rms} = \sqrt{(p_1)^2_{avg} + (p_2)^2_{avg}} \tag{2.14}$$

in which p_{rms} is the root-mean-square pressure of the complex wave shown in Figure 2.9c.

Equation 2.13 is important when we wish to determine the effect of adding two or more sound waves simultaneously. Consequently, we shall be referring to Equation 2.13 again. Normally we measure root-mean-square sound pressure levels of complex waves with sound level meters instead of measuring the peak pressures of the wave.

2.9 Sound Spectra

An acoustic spectrum plot is a graphical display of the frequency characteristics of a sound. For example, referring to Figure 2.9c, we know that there are only two frequencies present, ω_1 and ω_2, which form this complex sound wave. In this case the spectrum plot would appear as in Figure 2.10.

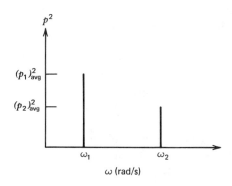

FIGURE 2.10   Acoustic spectrum plot of the complex wave on Figure 2.9c.

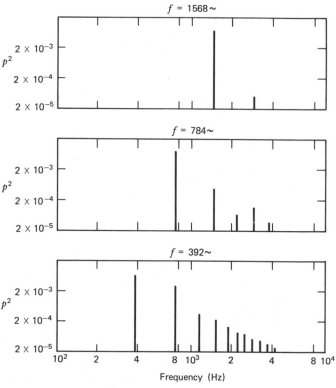

FIGURE 2.11 *Acoustic spectrum plot of three notes from a flute. (Source. H. F.*
Olson, Music, Physics, and Engineering, second edition, Dover, N.Y.)

Here the ordinate axis is chosen to be the mean square pressure of each tone
that forms the complex wave, and the abscissa axis represents the frequency.
Since there are only two frequencies present in the sound, only two points
are plotted in Figure 2.10.

Musical notes are interesting examples of sound waves that contain
several pure tones that are multiples of each other. The lowest frequency
component of a note is called the fundamental frequency, while the higher
frequencies are called the harmonics or the overtones. Figure 2.11 shows the
acoustic spectra of three notes from a flute. The spectra show that in the case
of these particular musical notes, the acoustic energy is primarily contained
in the fundamental frequency. Some acoustic spectra of musical notes on the
piano are shown in Figure 2.12, displaying a varying energy distribution
with the frequencies.

Most sounds that we hear in everyday life contain a multitude of frequencies. Sounds such as the running of water from a faucet, the hissing of
boiling water, and the sounds from a car engine contain a continuous

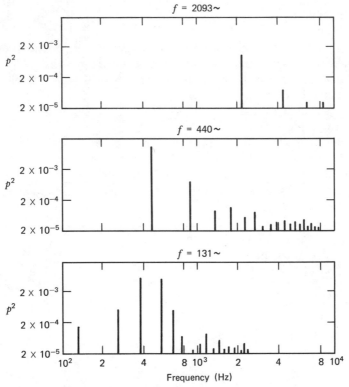

FIGURE 2.12 *Acoustic spectrum plot of three notes from a piano. (Source. H. F. Olson, Music, Physics & Engineering, second edition, Dover, N.Y.)*

spectrum of frequencies. Examples of continuous spectrum plots are shown in Figure 2.13. Such information is helpful in establishing the frequency distribution of the sound energy. Spectrum analysis is important to designers who wish to avoid harmful or annoying sounds that might otherwise be present in their finished products. In a later section we examine the types of equipment available for making spectrum analyses of complex sounds.

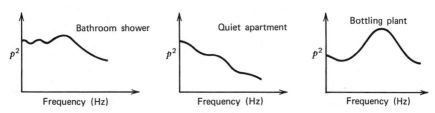

FIGURE 2.13 *Examples of continuous acoustic spectrum plots of everyday sounds.*

2.10 **Summary**

    A. The important ideas:

        1. As sound waves travel through air, the air particles experience pressure fluctuations about the undisturbed atmospheric pressure.

        2. Sound waves may be plane waves or spherical waves; freely progressing or obstructed.

        3. The period of a sound wave equals the time it takes for a sound wave to travel one wavelength.

        4. Sound waves travel in media containing mass and elasticity.

        5. The sound energy flow per unit area per unit time is called the sound intensity.

        6. The path of sound waves are altered by reflection, diffraction, and refraction.

        7. Spectrum analysis of sound waves displays the distribution of acoustic energy as a function of frequency.

    B. The important equations:

        1. $c = 20\sqrt{K}$ (2.2)

        2. $c = \lambda f$ (2.6)

        3. $I = \dfrac{W}{4\pi r^2}$ (2.8)

        4. $I = \dfrac{p^2}{\rho c}$ (2.9)

        5. $p_{avg}^2 = (p_1)_{avg}^2 + (p_2)_{avg}^2$ (2.13)

2.11 **Assignments**

    2.1 How are the wavelength and period of a sound wave related to each other?

    2.2 How does a plane wave differ from a spherical wave?

    2.3 Find the speed of propagation in air for the following temperatures: (a) 40°F, (b) 100°C, (c) 200°F. (*Hint.* F = 32 + 1.8 C)

    2.4 Find the speed of propagation in air at the following temperatures: (a) 0°C, (b) 22°C, (c) 100°F.

    2.5 The speed of propagation of a rod is measured at 3500 m/s. If the density of the material is 10,000 kg/m^3, what is Young's modulus E?

    2.6 During a fireworks display, it takes 0.4 s between the initial flash of a display and the sound reaching an observer. What was the distance between the observer and the ignited display if the air temperature was 22°C?

    2.7 At room temperature, the frequency of a sound wave is 2500 Hz. (a) What is the corresponding wavelength? (b) If the frequency is reduced to 1250 Hz, what is the wavelength?

2.8 Calculate the frequency of a sound wave at room temperature for the following wavelengths: (a) 1 m, (b) 1 ft, (c) 10 m.

2.9 Calculate the acoustic intensity of a spherical wave from a source of 10 W at a distance of (a) 3 m, (b) 6 m, and (c) 12 m.

2.10 At room temperature (22°C) and normal atmospheric pressure (0.751 m of Hg) the density of air equals 1.18 kg/m^3 and the speed of propagation equals 344 m/s. For this condition, calculate the acoustic intensity for a sinusoidal free progressive wave of peak pressure equal to 1.5 Pa.

2.11 What is meant by the inverse square law of the sound intensity?

2.12 Calculate the acoustic intensity of a spherical wave from a source of 50 W at a distance of (a) 3 m, and (b) 6 m.

2.13 At 3 m from a sound source the root-mean-square pressure is measured as 0.632 Pa. Assuming a point source, room temperature, and atmospheric pressure, calculate the sound power.

2.14 Sketch three successive reflections of the sound ray in Figure 2.14.

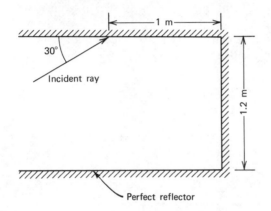

FIGURE 2.14   Problem 2.14.

2.15 Sketch four successive reflections of the sound ray in Figure 2.15.

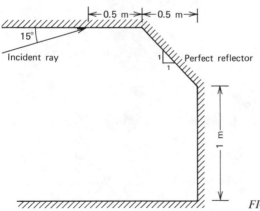

FIGURE 2.15   Problem 2.15.

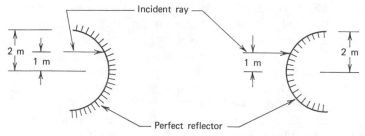

FIGURE 2.16   Problem 2.16.

2.16 Sketch the reflected ray for each condition shown in Figure 2.16.

2.17 What is meant by the diffraction of sound waves?

2.18 How does refraction of sound waves occur?

2.19 Explain how sound energy is dissipated by acoustic tile.

2.20 If $p = 50 \sin 2\pi ft + 20 \sin 4\pi ft$ and $f = 100$ Hz, sketch p versus t up to $t = 0.01$ s.

2.21 If $p = 25 \sin 2\pi ft + 20 \sin 4\pi ft + 15 \sin 6\pi ft$, calculate p_{rms}.

2.22 Plot the spectrum p^2_{avg} versus frequency for $p = \sum_{i=1}^{4} (40/i) \cos(i2\pi ft)$ if $f = 150$ Hz.

Suggested Reading List

D. F. Anthrop, *Noise Pollution*, Lexington Books, 1973.

W. Burns, *Noise and Man*, J. B. Lippincott, 1973.

L. L. Doelle, *Environmental Acoustics*, McGraw-Hill, 1972.

R. Taylor, *Noise*, Penguin Books, 1970.

T. Berland, *The Fight for Quiet*, Prentice-Hall, 1970.

R. A. Baron, *The Tyranny of Noise*, Harper and Row, 1970.

3
ANALYSIS OF SOUND WAVES

The sound pressure oscillations that our ears are capable of hearing generally represent very small pressure variations about the atmospheric pressure. From hearing tests it has been agreed that the lowest audible pressure from a 1000 Hz pure tone corresponds to 2×10^{-5} Pa. On the other hand, the pressure associated with the sensation of pain is approximately 200 Pa. Because of this rather large range in the magnitude of these numbers, the concept of the decibel (dB) is introduced in this chapter. The decibel essentially compresses this large range of numbers into a more meaningful scale. However, once we introduce the decibel as a measure of sound pressure, we must learn how to add multiple sound sources when each source is expressed in decibels. The acoustic spectrum analysis is also developed in this chapter by way of octave band analysis.

3.1 Definition of the Decibel

The decibel of the quantity A relative to (re) the quantity A_o is defined as

$$\text{decibel} = 10 \log \left(\frac{A}{A_o} \right), \qquad \text{dB re } A_o \tag{3.1}$$

The decibel is used in environmental noise pollution as a measure of sound power level, sound intensity level, and sound pressure level. Note that in each case the term "level" is synonymous with the decibel.

(A) The decibel for sound power level is defined as:

$$\text{sound power level,} \qquad L_w = 10 \log \left(\frac{W}{W_o} \right), \qquad \text{dB re } W_o \tag{3.2}$$

in which W = sound power in watts of a given source

W_o = reference sound power, generally 10^{-12} W

TABLE 3.1
Relationships Between Sound Power and Sound Power Level

Sound Power (W)	Sound Power Level (dB re 10^{-12} W)	Source
1,000	150	
100	140	
10	130	75-piece orchestra
1	120	
0.1	110	Auto on highway
0.01	100	
0.001	90	Voice shouting
0.0001	80	

Table 3.1 shows the range of sound power in watts, the corresponding sound power level, and some common sources that generate the power levels. We observe from the table that a 10-dB increase in power level corresponds to the power increasing by a factor of 10.

(B) The decibel for sound intensity level is defined as:

$$\text{sound intensity level,} \quad L_I = 10 \log \left(\frac{I}{I_o} \right), \quad \text{dB re } I_o \quad (3.3)$$

in which I = sound intensity in watts per square meter

I_o = reference sound intensity, generally 10^{-12} W/m^2

(C) The most common decibel scale used is the sound pressure level, which is measured directly on a sound level meter. Since the sound pressure squared is proportional to the sound intensity, as given earlier by Equation 2.9, we have the following definition.

$$\text{sound pressure level,} \quad L_p = 10 \log \left(\frac{p^2}{p_0^2} \right), \quad \text{dB re } p_o \quad (3.4)$$

in which p = root-mean-square sound pressure in Pascals

p_o = reference root-mean-square sound pressure,
generally 2×10^{-5} Pa

Table 3.2 lists the sound pressure magnitudes and the corresponding sound pressure levels for some familiar everyday sounds. We observe in this case that an increase of 20 dB in sound pressure level corresponds to the sound pressure increasing by a factor of 10.

Example 3.1

If the sound intensity level increases from 80 dB to 83 dB, what is the percentage change in the sound intensity?

From Equation 3.3, $L_I = 10 \log(I/I_o)$.

TABLE 3.2
Relationships Between Sound Pressure and Sound Pressure Level

Sound Pressure (Pa)	Sound Pressure Level (dB re 2×10^{-5} Pa)	Source
6.32	110	Near elevated train
2.00	100	Bottling plant
0.632	90	Full symphony
0.200	80	Inside automobile
0.0632	70	City street corner
0.0200	60	Conversational speech
0.00632	50	Typical office
0.00200	40	Living room
0.000632	30	Bedroom at night

Thus, for the two levels given,

$$\frac{I_1}{I_o} = \text{antilog}\left(\frac{80}{10}\right) = 1.0 \times 10^8$$

$$\frac{I_2}{I_o} = \text{antilog}\left(\frac{83}{10}\right) = 2.0 \times 10^8$$

To find the percentage change in sound intensity, we have the following relationship.

$$\frac{I_2 - I_1}{I_1} \times 100 = \frac{2.0 \times 10^8 - 1.0 \times 10^8}{1.0 \times 10^8} \times 100 = 100\% \quad \text{Answer}$$

In general, we can show that if the sound intensity doubles, the sound intensity level increases by 3 dB. Likewise, if the sound intensity level decreases by 3 dB, the sound intensity is halved.

3.2 Relationships Between Sound Power, Sound Intensity, and Sound Pressure Levels

If we assume a sound wave traveling as a free progressive wave, Equation 2.9 is valid.

$$I = \frac{p^2}{\rho c} \tag{2.9}$$

Substituting this expression for the intensity term in Equation 3.3, we have

$$L_I = 10 \log\left(\frac{p^2}{\rho c I_o}\right) \tag{3.5}$$

For standard atmospheric conditions, $\rho c = 406$ kg/(m²-s), so that Equation 3.5 reduces approximately to the following expression, provided $I_o = 10^{-2}$ W/m².

$$L_I = L_p \qquad (3.6)$$

We can say that subject to the above conditions the sound intensity level and the sound pressure level are, for all practical purposes, equal in magnitude to each other.

Likewise, if we start with the definition of the sound power level as given by Equation 3.2 and use Equation 2.7, it follows that

$$L_w = 10 \log \left(\frac{W}{W_o}\right) = 10 \log \left(\frac{IS}{I_o S_o}\right) = 10 \log \left(\frac{I}{I_o}\right) + 10 \log \left(\frac{S}{S_o}\right)$$

in which S = surface area of a sphere in square meters
$\qquad S_o$ = reference area of 1 m²

Thus,

$$L_w = L_I + 10 \log S \qquad (3.7)$$

From this relationship, we can calculate the sound power level of a sound source emanating free progressive spherical waves if the sound intensity level is known (or the sound pressure level is measured) and the radius of the spherical surface is known. This is the basis for one of the methods used to establish the sound power level of a source. Here the source is located in an anechoic chamber, an echo-free room, and measurements are made at selected points on a hypothetical sphere. By averaging the sound pressure level readings to account for directional effects from the source, the sound power level is calculated by means of Equation 3.7.

Example 3.2

Assume that a point source develops free progressive waves. At 6 m from the source, the sound pressure level is 80 dB. What is the sound power level of the source?

From Equation 3.6,

$$L_I = L_p = 80 \text{ dB}$$

Now the radius of the spherical surface is 6 m, so tha

$$S = 4\pi r^2 = 4(3.14)(6)^2 = 452 \text{ m}^2$$

Substituting into Equation 3.7,

$$\begin{aligned} L_w &= L_I + 10 \log S \\ &= 80 + 10 \log 452 = 80 + 10(2.655) \\ &= 106.6 \text{ dB} \qquad \text{Answer} \end{aligned}$$

3.3 Multiple Sound Sources

Suppose the sound pressure level of a source measures 80 dB on a sound level meter. Imagine that there is a second sound source operating alone that provides a reading of 80 dB on the same meter. What will the meter read if both sound sources are operating simultaneously? The answer is *not* 160 dB but, instead, 83 dB. To prove this, we recall Equation 2.13, which showed that the resulting mean-squared pressure was equal to the summation of the mean-squared pressures of the tones that made up the total sound. This idea can be extended to complex sound waves, each of which contains a mean-squared pressure of the overall complex wave. For the example under discussion, we calculate the p^2 values for each source, add them as indicated by Equation 2.13, and then calculate the final sound pressure level. Thus, for one sound source,

$$L_p = L_1 = 10 \log \left(\frac{p_1{}^2}{p_o{}^2} \right)$$

Here the subscript p is replaced by 1 to refer to the sound pressure level of source 1. Rearranging terms in this equation, we have

$$\frac{p_1{}^2}{p_o{}^2} = \text{antilog} \left(\frac{L_1}{10} \right) = 10^{L_1/10}$$

In this case, $L_1 = 80$ dB, so that

$$\frac{p_1{}^2}{p_o{}^2} = 1.0 \times 10^8$$

Likewise, for the second sound source,

$$\frac{p_2{}^2}{p_o{}^2} = 1.0 \times 10^8$$

Dividing both sides of Equation 2.13 by $p_o{}^2$ and introducing the above values, we obtain the following relationship.

$$\frac{p_{avg}^2}{p_o{}^2} = \frac{p_1{}^2}{p_o{}^2} + \frac{p_2{}^2}{p_o{}^2} = 2.0 \times 10^8$$

Finally, the total sound pressure level when both sound sources are operating simultaneously is obtained by substituting $p_{avg}^2/p_o{}^2$ into Equation 3.4 as follows.

$$L_p = 10 \log(2 \times 10^8) = 83 \text{ dB}$$

Consequently, we see that 80 dB plus 80 dB equals 83 dB.

Of course, this approach can be extended to several sound sources acting simultaneously. For example, if there are n sources operating together,

$$\frac{p_{avg}^2}{p_o^2} = \sum_{i=1}^{n} \frac{p_i^2}{p_o^2} = \sum_{i=1}^{n} 10^{L_i/10} \tag{3.8}$$

in which p_i is the root-mean-square pressure associated with sound source i and L_i is the corresponding sound pressure level.

Example 3.3

If individual sources $A = 90$ dB, $B = 80$ dB, and $C = 70$ dB, find L_p when all sources operate simultaneously.

First we calculate the squared pressure ratios for each source.

$$\frac{p_A^2}{p_o^2} = \text{antilog } 9 = 100 \times 10^7$$

$$\frac{p_B^2}{p_o^2} = \text{antilog } 8 = 10 \times 10^7$$

$$\frac{p_C^2}{p_o^2} = \text{antilog } 7 = 1 \times 10^7$$

Summing by Equation 3.8,

$$\frac{p_{avg}^2}{p_o^2} = 111 \times 10^7$$

Therefore, substituting into Equation 3.4, we have:

$$L_p = 10 \log(111 \times 10^7) = 10 \log(1.11) + 90$$
$$= 10(0.045) + 90 = 90.5 \text{ dB} \qquad \text{Answer}$$

It is noted that source A dominates in the calculation, while source C contributes slightly to the total sound pressure level. This leads us to the observation that if we wish to lower the overall sound pressure level from several sources, we should identify and control the major noise sources first, before concerning ourselves with those sources producing lower sound pressure levels.

Figure 3.1 is helpful in adding sound pressure levels two at a time. To add two sound levels, use the abscissa axis to locate the difference in the sound pressure levels, $(L_2 - L_1)$, between the two sources. Then read the corresponding ordinate value ΔL dB from the curve. The value ΔL is added to the larger of the two original sound pressure levels. This calculated value gives the combined sound pressure level. For example, in the case of the two sources each equal to 80 dB, $(L_2 - L_1) = 0$, and from the curve in Figure 3.1, $\Delta L = 3$ dB. Consequently, the combined $L_p = 83$ dB. In Example 3.3, first combine $C = 70$ dB with $B = 80$ dB. From the curve, $\Delta L = 0.4$ dB.

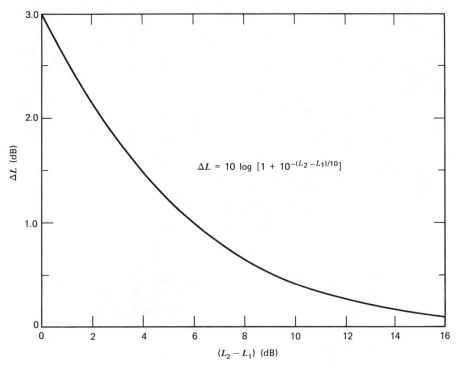

$$\Delta L = 10 \log [1 + 10^{-(L_2 - L_1)/10}]$$

FIGURE 3.1   Curve for adding sound pressure levels two at a time.

Thus, $C + B = 80.4$ dB. To combine this result with $A, (L_2 - L_1) = 9.6$ dB, which gives $\Delta L = 0.5$ dB to be added to the larger level. In this case, $L_p = 90.5$ dB, which agrees with the earlier answer in Example 3.3.

Generally, if $(L_2 - L_1)$ is greater than 10 dB, we may neglect the effect of the lower sound source, so that the combined L_p equals approximately the larger of the two sources.

As a final comment on multiple sound sources, we observe that there always exists sound before a machine is turned on. This is called the *background* noise level. When we measure the sound produced by the machine, we are in effect measuring both the background noise plus the machine sound. Consequently, to obtain the machine sound pressure level, we should subtract the background sound pressure level from the measured level when the machine is operating.

Example 3.4
The sound pressure level in a room is 65 dB before an air conditioner is turned on. With the air conditioner operating, the sound pressure level is 72 dB. What is the sound pressure level due to the air conditioner alone?

In this case,

$$\frac{p_{avg}^2}{p_o^2} = \text{antilog } 7.2 = 1.585 \times 10^7$$

For the background noise,

$$\frac{p_1^2}{p_o^2} = \text{antilog } 6.5 = 0.316 \times 10^7$$

For the air conditioner alone,

$$\frac{p_2^2}{p_o^2} = \frac{p_{avg}^2}{p_o^2} - \frac{p_1^2}{p_o^2}$$

$$= 1.585 \times 10^7 - 0.316 \times 10^7 = 1.269 \times 10^7$$

Therefore, the sound pressure level for the air conditioner is

$$L_p = 10 \log(1.269 \times 10^7) = 71.0 \text{ dB} \qquad \text{Answer}$$

This problem may also be solved graphically by means of Figure 3.2. In this case, L_p is the sound pressure level caused by the background noise plus the machine noise, while L_1 refers to the background noise only. The difference between these two quantities is plotted along the abscissa axis. The

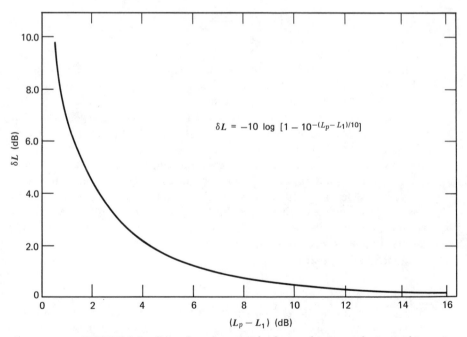

FIGURE 3.2   *Curve for subtracting background noise to obtain machine noise.*

term δL, which is plotted on the ordinate axis, refers to the number of decibels to be subtracted from L_p to establish the machine noise, L_2. In Example 3.4, $L_p = 72$ dB, and $L_1 = 65$ dB. Entering Figure 3.2 with $(L_p - L_1) = 7$ dB, we obtain δL equal to approximately unity. Hence, the machine noise $L_2 = 72 - 1 = 71$ dB, which agrees with the earlier result.

3.4 Octave Band Analysis

It was mentioned in Chapter 2 that we are frequently interested in knowing how sound energy is distributed as a function of the sound frequency. To accomplish this, the measured acoustic energy, or the equivalent mean-square pressure, can be electronically filtered into contiguous frequency bands. For each frequency band we measure the overall sound pressure level of the filtered sound within the band. The octave band is a common contiguous band used in the study of environmental noise pollution. Here the upper frequency limit of a band is twice that of the lower frequency limit. Thus, if f_l and f_u are the lower and upper frequency limits of an octave band, respectively, then

$$f_u = 2f_l \tag{3.9}$$

Since it is conventional to use a logarithmic scale for plotting frequencies, the average or center frequency, f_c, between the lower and upper frequency limits of an octave band is

$$\log f_c = \tfrac{1}{2}(\log f_l + \log f_u) = \log(f_l f_u)^{1/2}$$

Therefore,

$$f_c = \sqrt{f_l f_u} = \sqrt{2} f_l \tag{3.10}$$

The current set of octave bands used with modern acoustic instrumentation is shown in Table 3.3.

The octave band sound pressure level in decibels represents a measure of the mean-squared pressure of the sounds within the particular frequency band. Figure 3.3 shows an example of measured octave band data for a hair dryer. As already mentioned, the frequency on the abscissa axis is represented with a logarithmic scale. Also, as a matter of convention, the octave band decibel levels are plotted at the corresponding center frequency as seen

TABLE 3.3
Lower, Upper, and Center Frequencies of Modern Octave Bands

Lower frequency, f_l	44	88	177	355	710	1420	2840	5680
Upper frequency, f_u	88	177	355	710	1420	2840	5680	11360
Center frequency, f_c	63	125	250	500	1000	2000	4000	8000

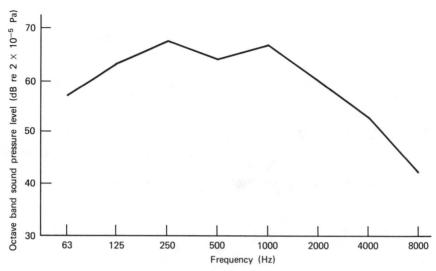

FIGURE 3.3   1/1 Octave band sound spectrum for a hair dryer.

in Figure 3.3. Finally, straight lines join the decibel levels to display the spectrum data. Figure 3.4 shows another example of octave band analysis of the sound from the interior of a small aircraft flying under normal cruising conditions.

As a final comment on octave band analysis, we note that the sound pressure levels in each band may be added to yield the total sound pressure

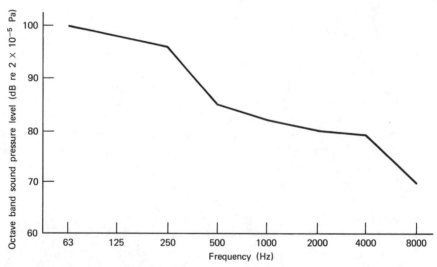

FIGURE 3.4   1/1 Octave band sound spectrum for the interior of a small aircraft flying under normal cruising conditions.

level associated with the sound source. We view each band level as a separate source and add all levels, as we did in the case of multiple sources described earlier. The following example demonstrates this point.

Example 3.5
Calculate the overall sound pressure level for the octave band data shown in Figure 3.4.

For systematic results, arrange the data in ascending order. Then combine the band sound pressure levels two at a time, using Figure 3.1.

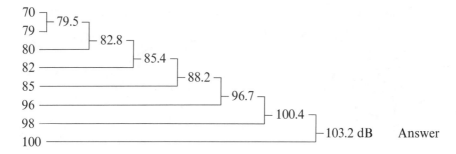

Thus, a sound level meter would measure approximately 103 dB as the overall sound pressure level inside the aircraft.

3.5 Other Frequency Spectrum Analyses

The octave bands described above are called 1/1 octaves. For a more detailed analysis of a sound wave, finer sets of contiguous bands are available, such as 1/2 octave bands and 1/3 octave bands. Table 3.4 demonstrates the division of a 1/1 octave band into these finer bands, all of which are called

TABLE 3.4
Relationships Between 1/1, 1/2, and 1/3 Octave Band Frequency Band Widths

Octave Analyzer	Logarithmic Band Width	Frequency Relationships
1/1	$\vdash\!\!\!\!\!\overset{\displaystyle f_l}{\rule{0pt}{0pt}}\!\!\!\!\!\underset{\displaystyle f_u}{\rule{0pt}{0pt}}\!\!\!\!\!\dashv$	$f_u = 2f_l$
1/2	$f_l \quad f_{u1} \quad f_u$	$f_{u1} = 2^{1/2}f_l$ $f_u = 2^{1/2}f_{u1} = (2^{1/2})(2^{1/2}f_l)$ $= 2f_l$
1/3	$f_l \quad f_{u1} \quad f_{u2} \quad f_u$	$f_{u1} = 2^{1/3}f_l$ $f_{u2} = 2^{1/3}f_{u1} = 2^{2/3}f_l$ $f_u = 2^{1/3}f_{u2} = 2f_l$

constant-percentage frequency bands. In the case of a 1/2 octave band analyzer, we obtain twice as many data points over the 1/1 octave band analyzer. For the 1/3 octave band analyzer, we have three times as many data points, which provides a finer filtering process of the sound. For example, Figure 3.5 shows both the 1/1 and the 1/3 octave band data for the hair dryer shown in Figure 3.3. Here we observe that the 1/3 octave band analyzer provides a sharper set of peaks and valleys in the plotted data.

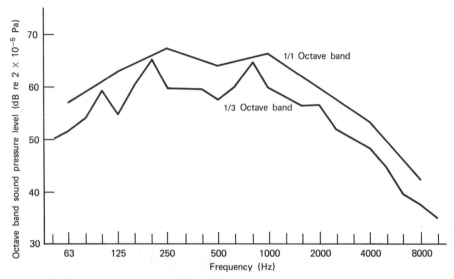

FIGURE 3.5   1/1 and 1/3 Octave band sound spectra of a hair dryer.

In addition to constant-percentage frequency band analyzers, there are also analyzers that use constant-frequency intervals throughout the desired frequency range. For example, if we wish to analyze a sound over the frequency range from 20 Hz to 10,000 Hz in constant intervals of 10 Hz, we would accumulate a total of 998 data points. This type of analysis is usually used in controlled laboratory tests and is helpful in locating dominant whinning sounds or narrow band energy sources being emitted by a machine. Such refined measurements aid the designer in eliminating undesirable sounds associated with a product.

3.6 Summary

A. The important ideas:
   1. The decibel is a logarithmic measurement for sound power level, sound intensity level, and sound pressure level.

2. Subject to ideal conditions, the sound intensity level is approximately equal to the sound pressure level.
3. If the sound intensity doubles, the sound intensity level increases by 3 dB; if it is halved, the sound intensity level decreases by 3 dB.
4. In adding decibel levels from multiple sources, first convert each value to its antilogarithm, add the results, and then calculate the overall decibel level.
5. When measuring machine noise, the background noise level should always be taken into consideration.
6. 1/1 octave band analysis is useful in establishing the sound energy distribution with frequency. Finer analyses may be obtained using 1/2 or 1/3 octave bands.

B. The important equations:

1. $L_w = 10 \log \left(\dfrac{W}{W_o} \right),$ dB re W_o

$$ (3.2) $$

2. $L_I = 10 \log \left(\dfrac{I}{I_o} \right),$ dB re I_o

$$ (3.3) $$

3. $L_p = 10 \log \left(\dfrac{p^2}{p_o{}^2} \right),$ dB re p_o

$$ (3.4) $$

4. $L_w = L_I + 10 \log S$

$$ (3.7) $$

5. $\dfrac{p_{avg}^2}{p_o{}^2} = \displaystyle\sum_{i=1}^{n} \dfrac{p_i^2}{p_o{}^2} = \sum_{i=1}^{n} 10^{L_i/10}$

$$ (3.8) $$

6. $f_u = 2f_l$

$$ (3.9) $$

7. $f_c = \sqrt{2} f_l$

$$ (3.10) $$

3.7 Assignments

3.1 Identify the three sound levels measured in decibels and define each.

3.2 If the sound power level is 125 dB for an appliance, what is the sound power in watts?

3.3 Calculate the sound power levels for: (a) 250 W, (b) 40 W, (c) 0.005 W.

3.4 Calculate the sound intensity level for: (a) 23 W/m^2, (b) 0.018 W/m^2.

3.5 If the sound pressure level equals 85 dB, what is the corresponding root-mean-square pressure?

3.6 As the distance from a point source doubles, show that the intensity level decreases by 6 dB.

3.7 The sound power from a point source is 30 W. What is the intensity level at (a) 5 m, (b) 10 m, (c) 20 m?

3.8 If the sound intensity doubles, show that the intensity level increases by 3 dB.

3.9 Derive Equation 3.6 starting with Equation 3.5.

3.10 At 4 m from a point source the sound pressure level is 92 dB. Assuming a free progressive spherical wave and standard atmospheric conditions, calculate the sound power level of the source.

3.11 What is meant by background noise? How was the equation in Figure 3.2 derived?

3.12 Why can't decibel values of separate sound sources be added arithmetically when all sources operate simultaneously?

3.13 A sound level meter registers 85 dB when source A runs separately, and it registers 87 dB when source B runs separately. What is the meter reading when both A and B run simultaneously? Solve algebraically and check your answer using Figure 3.1.

3.14 A sound level meter reads 83 dB when sources A and B are running simultaneously. If source A produces 81 dB separately, what is the individual sound pressure level of source B? Solve algebraically and check your answer using Figure 3.2.

3.15 In a plant individual noise sources produce the following sound pressure levels at a given station: $A = 91$ dB; $B = 88$ dB; $C = 92$ dB; and $D = 75$ dB.
(a) Calculate algebraically the sound pressure level when all noise sources operate simultaneously.
(b) Check your answer in part a by using Figure 3.1.

3.16 Company regulations limit factory sound pressure level exposure at 90 dB for an 8-h day. In a given factory, the current level of exposure is 88 dB. For this case, what is the maximum sound pressure level that a new machine may emit so as not to exceed the regulation?

3.17 A diesel-powered heavy truck has the following noise sources: straight-pipe exhaust—98 dB; fan—88 dB; engine—83 dB; air intake—75 dB; and other sources—75 dB. Calculate the total sound pressure level from the truck.

3.18 What is the purpose of octave band analysis and how are the octave band levels related to the overall sound pressure level?

3.19 Find the overall sound pressure level for the octave band data in Figure 3.3. Use Figure 3.1 for convenience.

3.20 Repeat problem 3.19 using the 1/3 octave band data in Figure 3.5.

3.21 Referring to Tables 3.3 and 3.4, establish the 1/2 octave band center frequency from 125 Hz to 250 Hz.

3.22 Referring to Tables 3.3 and 3.4, establish the 1/3 octave band center frequencies from 125 Hz to 250 Hz.

4
MEASURING SOUNDS

It is important that equipment be carefully selected to monitor and measure sounds. The type of sound and the required measurement accuracy dictate the particular equipment choosen for each situation. For example, we should know if the sound level remains fairly constant (steady-state sound), if the sound level fluctuates widely (intermittant sound), or if the sound includes sharp changes in sound pressure levels over short time intervals (impulse sound). Likewise, we need to know if weather conditions such as temperature, humidity, and wind might be a factor; if precautions are necessary to measure unobstructed sound waves; and if the sounds should be taped for a permanent record or for future analysis. It should be known whether the equipment meets the specifications promulgated by national and international organizations such as the American National Standards Institute (ANSI), the International Organization for Standardization (ISO), and the International Electrotechnical Commission (IEC). This chapter introduces some basic sound measurement equipment used in environmental noise pollution. Also, the types of sound fields that exist around noise sources are examined along with recommended measurement procedures.

4.1 Sound Level Meter

The basic parts of most sound level meters include a microphone, amplifiers, weighting networks, and a display meter reading in decibels. Figure 4.1 shows a schematic diagram of these elements of the meter. At the microphone, the sound wave energy is converted into an electrical signal that is boosted in magnitude at the preamplifier. The electrical signal may be modified by the weighting network, followed by a further boosting in magnitude through the amplifier. The rectifier converts the electrical signal from alternating current

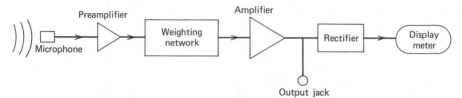

FIGURE 4.1   Schematic diagram of the basic parts of a sound level meter.

(a.c.) to direct current (d.c.) to cause the needle of the display meter to register the sound pressure level directly in decibels. The needle motion is controlled by a fast response or a slow response setting. The latter provides more damping to the needle motion and is normally desirable when the sound fluctuates appreciably. An output jack may exist to record or analyze the measured signal whenever desired. The elements shown in this figure are basic to most sound level meters, although individual types may vary somewhat in these features and in their capabilities. For example, digital readouts of the sound pressure level are gaining in popularity over the analog display meter.

Most sound level meters are designed as small hand-held instruments powered by dry cell batteries.[1,2] The capabilities of meters vary, depending on the particular specifications that the meter satisfies. In the United States, the American National Standard Specifications for Sound Level Meters, ANSI S 1.4—1971, is used by manufacturers to classify their sound level meters as follows.

Type 1—Precision Sound Level Meter.

Type 2—General Purpose Sound Level Meter.

Type 3—Survey Sound Level Meter.

Type S—Special Purpose Sound Level Meter.

Many community noise ordinances and laws governing occupational noise levels specify that measurements be made on at least a Type 2 sound level meter. Figure 4.2 shows two Type 1 sound level meters while Figure 4.3 shows three Type 2 sound level meters.

4.2 Microphones

There are three general types of microphones: the condenser microphone, the crystal or piezoelectric microphone, and the dynamic microphone. It is important to realize that the general characteristics of a microphone should be known before making any sound measurements. Some important features of a microphone include sensitivity, directional effects, decibel range, frequency range, and operating temperature range. No microphone will have outstanding qualities in all of these areas, so that compromises must be made in selecting a microphone. For example, as the dimensions of the microphone decrease, the frequency range increases while the sensitivity

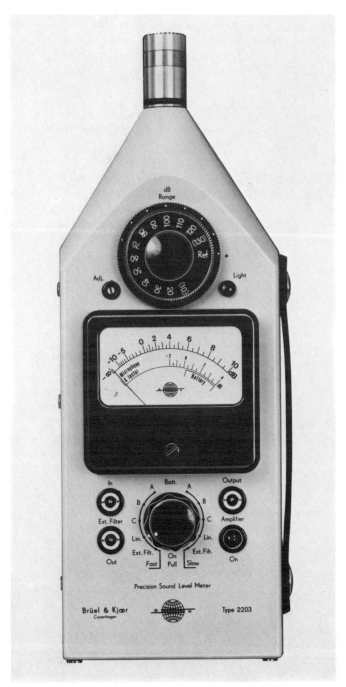

FIGURE 4.2   Type 1 sound level meters. (Courtesy of B & K Instruments, Inc. and General Radio Co.)

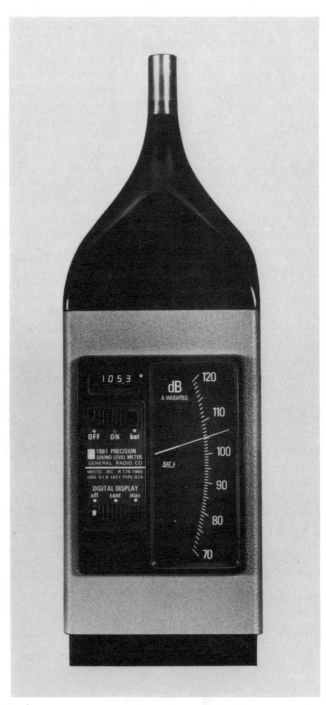

FIGURE 4.2 (Continued)

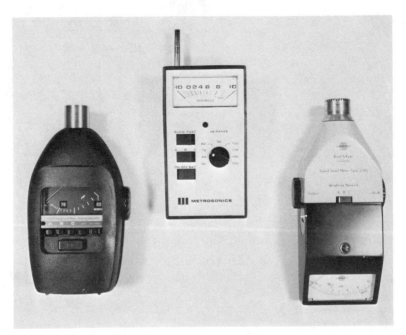

FIGURE 4.3   Type 2 sound level meters.

decreases. Most microphones used in field measurements in environmental noise pollution come in the following sizes based upon the microphone diameter: 1-in., 1/2-in., 1/4-in., and 1/8 in.

CONDENSER MICROPHONE. The operating principle of a condenser microphone involves an electrically charged diaphragm and backplate, as shown in Figure 4.4. The diaphragm and backplate act as electrodes of a capacitor charged by a polarizing voltage power supply so that when the diaphragm deflects under the sound pressure energy, the capacitance changes

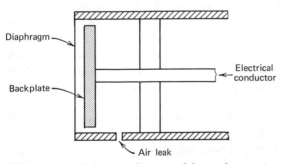

FIGURE 4.4   Schematic diagram of the condenser microphone.

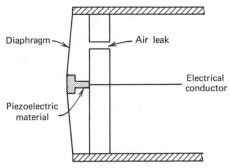

FIGURE 4.5   Schematic diagram of the piezoelectric microphone.

between these electrodes. Consequently, an electrical signal is developed in direct proportion to the movement of the diaphragm.

The electret microphone is a recently developed condenser microphone with an electrical charge permanently impregnated in the dielectric between the capacitor plates. This obviates the need for a separate polarizing voltage power supply, which is normally required in the traditional condenser microphone.

The condenser microphone is regarded as the most suitable transducer for measuring sound pressures in field measurements because of its flat linear response over its frequency range, high sensitivity, and long-term operational stability. Care should be exercised, however, when using this microphone in very humid situations, such as outdoor nighttime measurements in warm humid weather, so that water condensation does not develop on the backplate.

PIEZOELECTRIC MICROPHONE. This type of transducer utilizes crystals or dielectrics such as Rochelle salt, ammonium dihydrogen phosphate, and tourmaline, which convert the acoustic energy to electric energy. When the diaphragm in Figure 4.5 moves under the action of the sound waves, it produces a strain on the piezoelectric material, which has the property of generating an electrical charge in proportion to the strain magnitude. Consequently, the electrical signal so generated is directly related to the diaphragm motion.

While the piezoelectric microphone does not have characteristics as fine as the condenser microphone, it is a cheaper microphone of good quality. Water condensation on the backplate is not as much a problem, nor does it require a polarization voltage as in the case of the condenser microphone.

DYNAMIC MICROPHONE. The dynamic microphone generates an electrical signal developed by a moving coil in a magnetic field. Figure 4.6 shows a sketch of this microphone with the diaphragm undergoing motion from the sound waves. Dynamic microphones are used primarily in broadcast

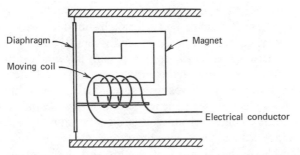

FIGURE 4.6   *Schematic diagram of the dynamic microphone.*

work and, consequently, are not normally used for measurements in environmental noise pollution. In any event, they should not be used around machines that have magnetic fields present.

4.3 Weighting Networks

The weighting networks in sound level meters attempt to alter the measured signal in a similar fashion as the human hearing mechanism. From the measured equal loudness level contours (see Chapter 6) the weighting network curves shown in Figure 4.7 were developed for the following conditions.

   A-weighting network: human response for low sound levels.

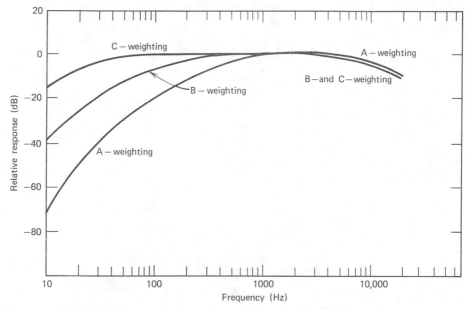

FIGURE 4.7   *Relative response of the A-, B-, and C-weighting networks.*

B-weighting network: human response for moderate sound levels.

C-weighting network: human response for high sound levels.

These weighting networks have been internationally standardized.

The A-weighting network has been adopted in many laws and ordinances to compensate for human hearing characteristics regardless of the sound intensity level. By examining the curves in Figure 4.7, we observe that the A-weighting network deletes low-frequency sound energy, while the C-weighting produces little change in the measured signal; that is, it provides a relatively flat response across the frequency range. Consequently, if the measured decibel levels on the A- and C-weighting networks are relatively close in value for a particular noise source, this means that there is little low-frequency energy present in the measured sound. On the other hand, if there is an appreciable difference between decibel levels from these two networks, then there is a significant amount of low-frequency energy generated by the noise source.

The D-weighting network shown in Figure 4.8 has been recommended as a correlation with human response from noise around airports. The A-weighting network is also shown in Figure 4.8 for comparison purposes. We observe that the D-weighting network does not delete as much low-frequency energy as the A-weighting network. Furthermore, it does boost the sound energy in the high-frequency range between 1000 and 12,000 Hz. Consequently, the D-weighted level of a noise source will always be higher than the

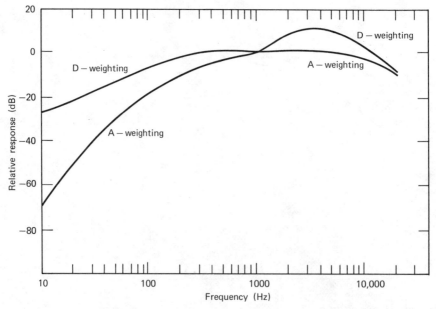

FIGURE 4.8 Relative response of the A- and D-weighting networks.

corresponding A-weighted level. Two points about the D-weighting network should be made. First, it has been developed from noise studies around airports only and, second, it has been proposed but not adopted by any international standards group, as in the case of the A, B, and C-weighting networks.

Readings on a weighting network should indicate the particular weighting network in use. For example, if we read 65 dB on the meter when using the A-weighting network, we record this as 65 dB(A) or simply 65 dBA. Similarly, if the reading is obtained with the C-weighting network, we would record it as 65 dB(C) or 65 dBC. Throughout this text the referred weighting network will be shown without the parentheses.

4.4 Auxiliary Equipment of the Sound Lever Meter

Some important auxiliary equipment that may be used with sound level meters is shown in Figure 4.9 and briefly described below.

CALIBRATOR. These are portable, battery-operated instruments that are used to calibrate a sound level meter. The calibration is a fairly straightforward procedure in which the calibrator is placed over the microphone of the sound level meter. A pure tone of known frequency and intensity level is generated by the calibrator and compared with the meter reading of the sound level meter. Adjustments are a simple matter and are made as required.

OCTAVE BAND FILTER SET. These filter sets are connected to a precision sound level meter for 1/1 or 1/3 octave band measurements. This arrangement is attractive for field measurements of steady-state noise, since the system is powered by dry cell batteries. It is a simple matter of selecting the center frequencies one at a time in the course of generating the octave band data. Normally octave band measurements do not modify the measured signal by weighting networks.

WIND SCREEN. Outdoor measurements should include a wind screen placed over the microphone of the sound level meter. This minimizes air flow turbulence around the diaphragm of the microphone. Generally, outdoor measurements are not recommended when the wind speed exceeds approximately 20 km/h. For example, the Society of Automotive Engineers (SAE) recommends a limit of 19 km/h (12 mi/h) wind speed when measuring noise at construction sites.

IMPULSE NETWORK. A precision sound level meter may include an impulse network to measure sounds whose pressure levels rise sharply for very short time intervals. A "hold" circuit may be available to record the maximum root-mean-square or maximum peak levels of the impulse sound.

SOUND LEVEL CALIBRATOR

PISTONPHONE

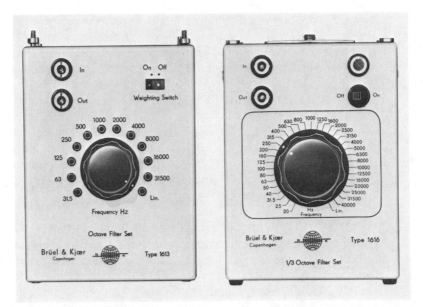

FIGURE 4.9   Some auxiliary equipment used with the sound level meter. (Courtesy of B & K Instruments, Inc.)

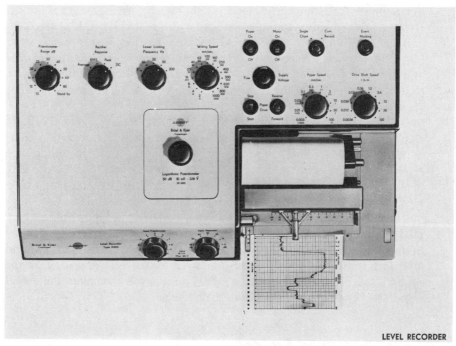

FIGURE 4.9 (Continued)

Readings from the impulse network may be labeled dBA(I), dBC(I), and so forth, depending on the weighting network used.

GRAPHIC LEVEL RECORDER. This instrument is used to provide a permanent graphic recording of measured sound level fluctuations over a period of time. The measured sound may come directly to the graphic level recorder from a sound level meter or from a tape recorder. It is also used extensively in analyzing measured sounds under laboratory conditions.

4.5 Tape Recording Sounds

Tape recorders are used in environmental noise pollution to provide a permanent storage of measured sounds. There are a variety of situations that preclude the use of a tape recorder when taking field measurements. Some of these include law suits that require playback of a disturbing noise for courtroom purposes, analysis of fluctuating or transient sounds such as aircraft flyover noise, and evaluation of impulse noise that might exist in a factory.

The output from a sound level meter is normally transmitted into the tape recorder. Whether the measured signal is passed through a weighting network or not will depend on its intended use. It is important that both the microphone of the sound level meter and the tape recorder be selected in such a way that they are of suitable quality for the particular task at hand. In particular, the tape recorder should not only be dependable, but it must have a flat frequency response, a wide dynamic range, and a minimum of wow and flutter.[2] In some cases it is desirable to be able to operate the tape recorder from either batteries or alternating current power and to have a variety of tape speeds.

There are two types of recording used in noise measurements: the direct recording (with high-frequency bias) and the frequency modulation technique. For ordinary analysis of the recorded data the direct recording tape recorder is more economical. For analysis of recorded sounds requiring phase preservation, such as impulse noise, and correlation analysis, a tape recorder with the frequency modulation capability is essential.

It will be necessary to record a reference signal on the tape before making field measurements with a tape recorder. This may be achieved by transmitting a signal from a calibrator, such as a pistonphone, through the sound level meter into the tape recorder. Knowing the attenuator setting on the sound level meter when recording actual noise levels thereafter, the actual sound level can be established from the reference level.

4.6 Types of Sound Fields

Free progressive waves have been described as sound waves that propagate without obstruction from the source to the receiver. In the case of spherical waves, the inverse square law applies so that as the distance is doubled from the source, the sound pressure level decays by 6 dB. In reality, this law does not apply at positions close to the sound source. Consequently, we distinguish between a near field and a far field when making sound measurements.

The *near field* is defined as that region close to the source where the inverse square law does not apply. Usually this region is located within a few wavelengths of the source, and it is also controlled by the dimensions of the source.

The *far field* may consist of two parts, the free part and the reverberant part. In the free part of the far field, the sound pressure level obeys the inverse square law. Such a situation exists in anechoic chambers, which are essentially echo-free rooms. In practice, this portion of the far field may be approximated as being several wavelengths from the source, or several times the circumference of the source, choosing whichever is larger. Note that this portion of the far field may exist for indoor and outdoor situations. The reverberant part of the far field exists for enclosed situations where the reflected sound waves are superimposed on the incident sound waves. If there are many reflected waves from all possible directions, a *diffuse sound field* exists in which the acoustic energy per unit volume is essentially uniform throughout the room. This situation is sometimes found in industrial plants.

When measuring sounds, it is necessary to realize what type of sound field exists. Sometimes we must make measurements in the near field while, on the other hand, there are situations where we wish to be so located from the source that the inverse square law holds. We should check with the manufacturer's recommended orientation of the sound level meter for measurements in the free part of the far field. In indoor situations, we can determine if a diffuse sound field exists by taking several readings on the sound level meter at various locations around the room. If the readings are essentially constant, we may assume that a diffuse sound field exists. In this case the sound level meter has no fixed orientation, since the sound arrives at the microphone from all directions in the room.

4.7 Recommended Measurement Procedures

It is recommended that care be exercised against reflected sound waves from the operator's body when using a sound level meter. Whenever possible, the sound level meter should be mounted on a tripod and the operator should be at least 0.5 m away from the nearest edge, as shown in Figure 4.10.[2] This procedure is especially important if the measured sound consists of free progressive waves or one in which a few dominant frequencies exist. As the noise environment approaches a diffuse sound field or one that contains a wide frequency distribution of energy (wide-band noise), this precaution against reflected sound waves from the presence of the operator may be relaxed.

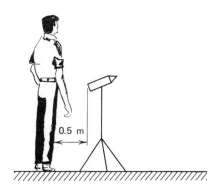

0.5 m

FIGURE 4.10 Operator position relative to a sound level meter mounted on a tripod.

Additional recommendations for measuring noise[3] include the following.

The sound level meter, satisfying ANSI or IEC criteria, is operated on the A-weighting network for fast response. Sound level measurements are made at the place and time of their occurrence and should not be extracted from measurements made nearby or at other times.

Outdoor measurements are made 1.2 to 1.5 m above the ground and, where practical, at least 3.5 m from reflecting surfaces such as buildings. Measurements that deviate from these recommended distances should be specified accordingly.

Indoor sound measurements should be made at least 1.2 to 1.5 m above the floor, at least 1 m from walls, and 1.5 m from windows. To account for the presence of standing waves, readings should be averaged arithmetically over ± 0.5 m about each of at least three positions. Measurements are normally made with windows closed unless they are regularly left open. If this is the case, measurements are made both with windows closed and windows open. If it is impractical to make indoor measurements, Table 4.1 provides approximate reductions in dBA levels from the outdoor levels to arrive at the indoor levels.

TABLE 4.1
Sound Level Reduction Due to Houses[a] **in Warm and Cold Climates, With Windows Open and Closed**

	Windows Open (dBA)	Windows Closed (dBA)
Warm climate	12	24
Cold climate	17	27
Approximate national average	15	25

Source. "Information on Levels of Environmental Noise Requisite to Protect Public Health and Welfare with an Adequate Margin of Safety," EPA, March 1974.
[a] Attenuation of outdoor noise by exterior shell of the house.

As a final comment on recommended measurement procedures, attention is drawn to the presence of background noise. By examining Figure 3.2 we observe that if the difference between background noise plus machine noise, L_p, and the background noise alone, L_1, exceeds 10 dB, then no background noise correction is needed. As the difference $(L_p - L_1)$ approaches 3 dB, it becomes desirable to relocate the machine to quieter surroundings if at all possible.

4.8 Initial Checklist

The following checklist includes the kinds of questions you should consider before making field measurements.

1. What national or international specifications must the equipment satisfy?
2. What calibration procedures are necessary?

3. How will the measurements be recorded and should they be weighted?
4. Where are the measurements to be made? At ear level, at a property boundary line, adjacent to a highway, under an airplane flight path?
5. What produces the major sound?
6. What is the nature of the noise? Impulse, steady-state, fluctuating? Are pure tones present?
7. When are these sounds operating? Daytime, nighttime, weekends?
8. What are the physical dimensions of the sound sources?
9. Are there unusual environmental conditions (temperature, humidity, wind, etc.)?
10. Will the measurements be made in the near field or the far field? Will they be made in the free part or the reverberant part of the far field?
11. If measurements will be made in the free part of the far field, what is the recommended orientation of the sound level meter for the particular type of microphone to be used?

4.9 Summary

The important ideas:
1. Microphones convert acoustic energy to electric energy.
2. Condenser microphones operate on the principle of a capacitor.
3. Piezoelectric microphones operate on the principle of electrical charges being generated because of strain on the piezoelectric material.
4. Dynamic microphones operate on the principal of a moving coil in a magnetic field generating an electric signal.
5. Weighting networks are intended to modify the measured sound to correlate with the way we hear.
6. The inverse square law holds in the free part of the far field.
7. Diffuse sound fields exist in the reverberant part of the far field in which the acoustic energy per unit volume is constant.
8. The presence of reflecting surfaces can produce significant errors when measuring free progressive sound waves or sounds containing a few dominant frequencies.

4.10 Assignments

4.1 List the types of sound level meters classified by the ANSI S 1.4—1971 specifications.

4.2 Sketch the basic parts of a sound level meter and explain the function of each part.

4.3 Explain the principle of operation of the condenser microphone. What is the special feature of the electret microphone?

4.4 Explain the principle of operation of the piezoelectric microphone.

4.5 Explain the principle of operation of the dynamic microphone.

4.6 Familiarize yourself with a sound level meter. What is its frequency range, decibel range? What type of microphone does it employ? What limitations exist with temperature range and humidity? What weighting networks are available? What type of sound level meter is it as designated by ANSI S 1.4—1971?

4.7 Perform the following steps with a sound level meter.
(a) Battery check.
(b) Calibration using a pistonphone or other calibrator.

4.8 Take a sound level meter and wind screen for a walking survey of indoor and outdoor sound sources. Record readings on both the A- and C-weighting networks. Describe the sound source and location of readings relative to the source, and record any other information you believe important. Write a brief summary of your activity.

4.9 Explain the meaning of the A-, B-, and C-weighting networks.

4.10 Discuss the meaning of the D-weighting network.

4.11 Explain what is meant by the following types of sound fields: near field, far field, diffuse sound field.

4.12 Set up a fan in the laboratory. Using a sound level meter, record the sound pressure levels at a distance of one meter in front and one meter to the side of the fan. Record readings using both the A- and C-weighting networks, with and without a wind screen. Write a brief summary of your data and observations.

4.13 Set up a noise source in the laboratory, say a bell. Using a sound level meter, try to establish the near field and far field. How well does the inverse square law hold?

4.14 What are the ISO recommended practices for making outdoor and indoor noise level measurements?

4.15 Familiarize yourself with the octave band filter set attached to a precision sound level meter. What limitations exist with this equipment as described by the manufacturer's catalog?

4.16 Using an octave band filter set, select at least one steady-state noise source for measurements. If possible, turn off the noise source to establish the spectrum sound pressure levels and the overall sound pressure level associated with the background noise. With the source operating, record octave band readings and the overall sound pressure level. Plot the data for each case and make corrections for background noise to establish the noise spectra and the overall sound pressure level of the noise source.

4.17 Referring to the spectrum data in Figure 3.3, calculate the overall dBA level using the A-weighting network curve for correction purposes. (For convenience, refer to the tabulated A-weighted values in Appendix A.)

4.18 Repeat problem 4.17 for the 1/3 octave band data in Figure 3.5.

4.19 Familiarize yourself with a tape recorder in the laboratory. Connect the output from a sound level meter to the input of the tape recorder. Connect the output of the tape recorder to the input of a graphic level recorder. Using a calibrator, record a reference signal on the tape and observe the graphic level recording of this signal. How can this reference signal be used?

References

[1] A. P. G. Peterson and E. E. Gross, Jr., *Handbook of Noise Measurement*, seventh edition, General Radio, 1974.

[2] J. T. Broch, *Acoustic Noise Measurements*, Bruel & Kjaer, 1971.

[3] ISO Recommendation R 1996, May 1971.

5

CONTROLLING SOUNDS

Efforts to control noise are usually aimed at lowering the sound intensity of the noise source. There are other situations where we want the receiver to hear speech or music that is loud and clear. This chapter introduces some aspects of controlling wanted and unwanted sounds. This includes an overview of the general noise control concepts in terms of the source-path-receiver view of the problem, an examination of the desirable properties of indoor sounds, the properties of sound absorption and sound transmission loss of materials, and the usefulness of vibration isolation mounts and noise barriers. We conclude by examining two practical noise reduction problems that show a variety of solutions and resulting decibel reductions.

5.1 **Source-Path-Receiver**

There are three ways to eliminate unwanted sounds: (1) eliminate the sound at the *source*, (2) modify the *path* along which the sound energy is transmitted, and (3) provide the *receiver* with some form of protection. The source-path-receiver forms a linkage system with which we can make attempts at controlling the noise. In some cases, controlling the noise at the source will be sufficient; in other cases it may be necessary to control the noise at each step of the system.

Generally, taking care of the noise problem at the source is the most desirable approach whenever practicable. Here we attempt to reduce the radiated acoustic power by introducing mufflers, vibration isolation mounts, vibration damping materials, reducing speed of operation, and so forth. For best results these efforts at controlling noise at the source should occur in the early design stages. Indeed, a decision in the early stages might be to choose a quieter machine over another. Such a step can save many problems, since later modifications may be costly and sometimes technically impractical.

Modification of the sound path includes obvious steps such as increasing the distance between the source and the receiver and orientating the source so that the radiated power directed at the receiver is a minimum. Other efforts incorporate sound barriers, absorptive materials such as acoustic tile, and complete enclosures of the sound source.

In situations where neither source modifications nor path modifications reduce the sound to acceptable levels, direct protection of the individual is necessary. In industrial situations, this includes rotating personnel from one room to another, issuing ear protection equipment, issuing personal noise dosimeters, and maintaining regular audiograms to monitor employees' hearing acuity. Personal ear protection equipment include ear muffs, ear plugs, and throw-away ear plug material. Small pocket-sized noise dosimeters can be worn to assess the risk of hearing loss as prescribed by federal and state regulations.

5.2 Hearing Indoor Sounds

When we listen to sounds in a room, we hear both the direct sound and the reflected sound. We wish to hear these sounds so that they are clear enough and loud enough. The amount of reflected sound should reinforce the direct sound to make it loud enough and, at the same time, there should be no echoes or noticeable overlapping in syllables or musical notes. The reverberation time of a room is the acoustic property that plays an important role in the enrichment of sound for the listening audience. It is known that the reverberation time should be long enough to enhance the blending of sounds, but short enough to avoid excessive overlapping and confusion.

Until the end of the nineteenth century, the acoustic design of halls and churches was largely an art practiced by architects and engineers. In 1895, the president of Harvard University was unhappy about the acoustics in a new building on the campus. He asked Wallace C. W. Sabine, at the time an assistant professor of physics, to "do something" about the situation. Sabine had little guidance from the literature on architectural acoustics, so he decided to make some measurements in the room using a pipe organ, stop watch, and his own good hearing. He measured how long it took for the sound from the pipe organ to decay when a given number of seat cushions were placed in the room, the seat cushions being highly absorptive of sound energy. That is, the more seat cushions present in the room, the shorter time was required for the sound to decay the same number of decibels. By repeating the test many times with different numbers of seat cushions placed throughout the room, Sabine developed the following equation, which to this day is used in acoustic room design.

TABLE 5.1
Recommended Reverberation Times for Music and Speech Rooms

	Reverberation Times (s)
Music	
Rehearsal rooms	0.80 to 1.00
Chamber music	1.00 to 1.50
Orchestral/choral/average church music	1.50 to 2.00
Large organ/liturgical choir	2.00 to 2.25
Speech	
Small offices	0.50 to 0.75
Classrooms/lecture rooms	0.75 to 1.00
Work rooms	1.00 to 2.00

Source. Sound Control Construction Principles and Performance, second edition. Copyright © 1972 by United States Gypsum Co.

$$T = 0.161 \frac{V}{a} \tag{5.1}$$

in which T = reverberation time, in seconds, to reduce the sound intensity from a level of 60 dB above the threshold of audibility to the threshold of audibility

V = room volume in cubic meters

a = sound absorption in sabins

Recommended reverberation times for best audible results are shown in Table 5.1. While this table conveniently lists the recommended reverberation times, there are sometimes conflicting demands on the architect to satisfy all interested parties. For example, the clergy may want the congregation in a cathedral to hear the prayers and sermons clearly, requiring one reverberation time, while the choir master wishes the music to resound fully, requiring a different reverberation time.

In any event, before we are able to apply Equation 5.1 to problems, we must examine the sound absorption of materials, as developed in the next section.

5.3 Sound Absorption

The sound absorption coefficient of a reflecting/absorbing surface is defined as the fraction of the energy absorbed during each reflection at a specific frequency. The process of sound absorption is a conversion of acoustic energy to thermal energy, which takes place on the material's surface. Further improvement in sound absorption occurs if there are air pockets close to the material's surface for the sound waves to travel around before

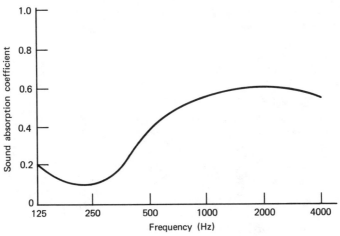

FIGURE 5.1   Sound absorption coefficient as a function of 1/3 octave band center frequencies.

reflecting back into the room. Surfaces that are primarily reflective include glass, metal, plaster, and other "hard" surfaces. Such materials have a sound absorption ≤ 0.05. On the other hand, porous materials such as acoustic tile, rugs, and draperies are primarily absorptive, so that the sound absorption coefficient approaches unity.

Figure 5.1 shows an example of the variation of the sound absorption coefficient with the frequency. We observe that the material absorbs more acoustic energy at some frequencies than at others. Some manufacturers provide simply the arithmetic average of the values of the sound absorption coefficients for frequencies at 250, 500, 1000, and 2000 Hz measured in 1/3 octave bands. The result is expressed as the noise reduction coefficient (NRC). For the data in Figure 5.1,

$$\text{NRC} = \tfrac{1}{4}(0.10 + 0.40 + 0.56 + 0.60) = 0.42$$

Standard laboratory test procedures as prescribed by the American Society for Testing Materials (ASTM C 423-66) should be followed by manufacturers in establishing sound absorption coefficients. In fact, the published coefficients are called the Sabine or effective sound absorption coefficients, α, since they are obtained using Equation 5.1 for a test setup in a specially designed highly reflective room called a reverberation room. Table 5.2 shows some representative values of effective absorption coefficients for commonly used materials.

If the sound absorption coefficient is known for each surface in a room, the sound absorption, a, in sabins, is found as follows.

$$a = \alpha_1 S_1 + \alpha_2 S_2 + \alpha_3 S_3 + \cdots$$

TABLE 5.2
Effective Absorption Coefficients

Material	Frequency (Hz)		
	125	500	2000
Acoustic paneling	0.16	0.50	0.80
Acoustic plaster	0.30	0.50	0.55
Brick wall, unpainted	0.02	0.03	0.05
Draperies, light	0.04	0.11	0.30
Draperies, heavy	0.10	0.50	0.82
Felt	0.13	0.56	0.65
Floor, concrete	0.01	0.02	0.02
Floor, wood	0.06	0.06	0.06
Floor, carpeted	0.11	0.37	0.27
Glass	0.04	0.05	0.05
Marble or glazed tile	0.01	0.01	0.02
Plaster	0.04	0.04	0.05
Rock wool	0.35	0.63	0.83
Wood paneling, pine	0.10	0.10	0.08

Listed values are only representative in that actual values also depend on mounting and thickness of the material.

Source. L. E. Kinsler and A. R. Frey, *Fundamentals of Acoustics*, Second edition, John Wiley & Sons, Inc., 1962, p. 435.

or, in summation form,

$$a = \sum_i \alpha_i S_i \qquad (5.2)$$

in which α_i = Sabine sound absorption coefficient of surface area i

S_i = area of surface i in square meters

The sabin is the unit for the sound absorption, a, where 1 sabin is the amount of sound absorbed by a theoretically perfect absorptive surface of area equal to 1 m². In Equation 5.2 we are adding the number of sabins for each absorbing surface in the room. It is important to realize that as the sound absorption increases, the sound intensity in the room decreases. If new acoustic materials introduced in a room doubles the sound absorption, the sound intensity level decreases by 3 dB. In practice, approximately 5 dB to 10 dB represents the reduction limit to be expected from absorbent materials from practical and economical considerations.[1,2]

The following expression[2] is used to approximate the reduction in the sound pressure level, in dB, due to additional sound absorption materials added to a room:

$$\text{Noise Reduction} = \text{NR} = 10 \log\left(\frac{a_o + a_a}{a_o}\right) \qquad (5.3)$$

in which

a_o = original absorption present in sabins

a_a = added absorption in sabins

In calculating a_a, care must be exercised that a reduced sound absorption coefficient be used in those cases where the added absorption material covers an existing surface. This is demonstrated in Example 5.2.

Example 5.1

Calculate the sound absorption and the reverberation time of a room with the following dimensions and Sabine sound absorption coefficients: length = 10 m; width = 7 m; height = 5 m; floor—carpeting, $\alpha = 0.20$; ceiling—painted concrete block, $\alpha = 0.07$; walls—wood, $\alpha = 0.07$.

First calculate the area of each surface with common sound absorption coefficients.

Area computation:

$$S_1 = \text{floor area} = 10(7) = 70 \text{ m}^2 \qquad\qquad \alpha_1 = 0.20$$
$$S_2 = \text{ceiling area} = 10(7) = 70 \text{ m}^2 \qquad\qquad \alpha_2 = 0.07$$
$$S_3 = \text{wall area} = 2(50 + 35) = 170 \text{ m}^2 \qquad \alpha_3 = 0.07$$

Using Equation 5.2,

$$a = 0.20(70) + 0.07(70) + 0.07(170) = 30.8 \text{ sabins} \qquad \text{Answer}$$

From Equation 5.1,

$$T = 0.161\,\frac{V}{a}$$

in which $V = 10(7)(5) = 350 \text{ m}^3$

$\qquad\qquad a = 30.8$ sabins

Therefore,

$$T = \frac{0.161(350)}{30.8} = 1.83 \text{ s} \qquad \text{Answer}$$

Example 5.2

Calculate the noise reduction for the room in Example 5.1 if the ceiling is covered with acoustical tile with a Sabine sound absorption coefficient equal to 0.6.

The noise reduction is given by equation (5.3),

$$NR = 10 \log \left(\frac{a_o + a_a}{a_o} \right) \tag{5.3}$$

in which $a_o = 30.8$ sabins as calculated in Problem 5.1.

Now

$$a_a = (0.60 - 0.07)(70)$$
$$= 37.1 \text{ sabins}$$

Note that a reduced sound absorption coefficient equal to 0.53 is used to account for the net absorption of the ceiling. Substituting into equation (5.3),

$$NR = 10 \log \left(\frac{30.8 + 37.1}{30.8} \right) = 3.4 \text{ dB} \qquad \text{Answer}$$

5.4 Sound Transmission Loss

Until now we have been considering the interior treatment of a room with sound absorbing material to produce desirable listening conditions. Another important aspect of sound control deals with keeping sounds from directly entering or leaving the room. This requires that the walls, floors, and ceiling have desirable sound transmission characteristics.

By definition, the sound transmission loss (STL) of a partition is

$$STL = 10 \log \left(\frac{I_i}{I_t} \right), \text{ dB}$$

in which $I_i =$ sound intensity incident on one surface of the partition in watts per square meter
$I_t =$ sound intensity radiated from the opposite surface of the partition in watts per square meter

The intensity I_t is less than I_i, since some of the incident energy is reflected back toward the source, while another portion is absorbed by the material of the partition.

The sound transmission loss is determined experimentally for a partition between two reverberation rooms[2] by the following expression.

$$STL = L_1 - L_2 + 10 \log \left(\frac{S}{a} \right) \tag{5.4}$$

in which $L_1 =$ time space average sound pressure level in the source room
$L_2 =$ time space average sound pressure level in the receiving room
$S =$ total radiating surface area of the partition in square meters

a = total sound absorption in the receiving room in sabins

The difference $(L_1 - L_2)$ is called the noise reduction of the partition.

If the partition is a rigid barrier with air on either side, it can be shown[3,4] that the sound transmission loss is described by what is called the field-incidence mass law.

$$STL = 20 \log wf - 47.4 \tag{5.5}$$

in which w = area density of the barrier in kilograms per square meter

f = frequency of the sound in Hertz

For example, a brick wall 0.3048 m thick has an area density equal to 590 kg/m^2. If the frequency of the incident sound is 500 Hz, then

$$STL = 20 \log(590)(500) - 47.4$$
$$= 109.4 - 47.4 = 62.0 \text{ dB}$$

We observe from Equation 5.5 that the predicted STL increases by 6 dB if the area density doubles or the sound frequency doubles.

As in the case of the sound absorption coefficient, the sound transmission loss of panels is found under strict test procedures prescribed by ASTM E 90-70. Figure 5.2 shows the sound transmission loss varying with frequency for a panel measured in 1/3 octave band intervals. It is common practice[5]

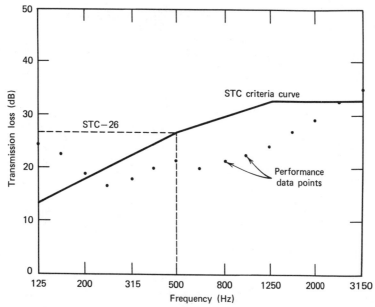

FIGURE 5.2 *Example of applying the STC criterion curve to performance data points to establish the STC rating of a material.*

to replace this curve by a single number and call it the sound transmission class (STC). This is accomplished by adjusting vertically the STC criterion curve shown in Figure 5.2 until the average of all data points below the criterion curve is no more than 2 dB, and no single data point on the test curve is more than 8 dB below the criterion curve. When so adjusted, the sound transmission loss at 500 Hz is taken off the criterion curve as the STC value. For the example shown in Figure 5.2, the STC value equals 26.

In addition to panels, STC values are available for a wide variety of wall and ceiling construction, doors, windows, and the like to insulate against sounds of speech, radio, television, and music. They should not be used for noise sources whose spectra are different from these sources. Sound isolation requirements for various types of occupancy that may contain these sounds are shown in Table 5.3 in terms of STC values. For example, an STC value of 60 is recommended for the wall construction between a bedroom and living room for the luxury class. Consequently, the wall construction to be used should have an STC rating of at least 60 for this case.

In addition to the direct airborne sound transmission through a partition as described above, noise may also follow paths either between the two adjacent rooms or through other walls, ceilings, and floors common to both rooms. This phenomenon is called airborne flanking noise, and typical

TABLE 5.3
Sound Transmission Class: Suggested Values for Typical Installations

Building Type	(Separate Occupancy Unless Noted) Room Under Consideration	Adjacent Room	Sound Transmission Class		
			Luxury	Average	Minimum
Residential,	Bedroom	Bedroom	55	50	45
including		Living room	60	55	50
motels,		Kitchen	60	55	50
hospitals,		Bathroom	60	55	50
and		Corridor	55	50	45
dormitories		Lobby	60	55	50
		Mechanical room	60+	60	55
		Room in same occupancy	50	45	40
	Living room	Living room	55	45	40
		Kitchen	60	50	45
		Bathroom	60	50	45
		Corridor	55	45	45
		Lobby	60	55	50
		Mechanical room	60+	60	50

TABLE 5.3 (*Continued*)

Building Type	(Separate Occupancy Unless Noted) Room Under Consideration	Adjacent Room	Sound Transmission Class		
			Luxury	Average	Minimum
	Kitchen or bathroom	Kitchen	50	45	40
		Bathroom	50	45	40
		Corridor	50	40	40
		Lobby	60	50	45
		Mechanical room	60+	55	45
Business	Office	Office	55	50	45
		General area	50	45	40
		Corridor	50	45	40
		Washroom	55	50	45
		Kitchen	55	50	45
		Conference room	55	50	45
	Conference room	General area	50	45	40
		Corridor	45	40	40
		Washroom	50	45	40
		Kitchen	55	50	45
		Conference room	50	45	40
	General area	Corridor	45	40	40
		Washroom	50	45	40
		Kitchen	55	50	45
School	Classroom	Classroom			45
		Laboratory			45
		Corridor			40
		Kitchen			50
		Shop			55
		Recreation area			45
		Music room			60
		Mechanical room			50
		Washroom			45
	Music room	Laboratory			45
		Corridor			45
		Shop			50
		Recreation area			50
		Music room			55
		Mechanical room			50

Note. Values in the "average" column will meet or exceed FHA requirements for low land-use intensity; values in the "minimum" column will meet or exceed requirements for high land-use intensity.

Source. Sound Control Construction Principles and Performance, second edition. Copyright © 1972 by United States Gypsum Co.

FIGURE 5.3   Flanking transmission of airborne noise. (Source. "A Guide to Airborne, Impact, and Structure Borne Noise," HUD, Washington, D.C., September 1967.)

examples in a residence are shown in Figure 5.3. Finally, flanking transmission of both impact noise and structure-borne noise, which are shown in Figure 5.4, are commonly found in residential dwellings. Here we observe the many noise sources and their interaction with the building structural elements so as to produce a variety of flanking phenomena.

5.5 Sound Attenuation by Barriers

Optical-diffraction theory[6] has been applied to establish the sound attenuation loss caused by the presence of a straight solid thin wall. For simplicity, we shall treat only the case in which a point source and receiver, shown in Figure 5.5, lie in the plane of the page. From the geometry, we first calculate the Fresnel number, N, given by

$$N = \frac{2(A + B - d)}{\lambda} \tag{5.6}$$

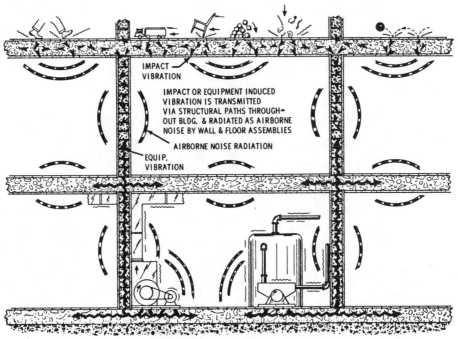

FIGURE 5.4 Flanking transmission of impact and structure-borne noise. (Source. "A Guide to Airborne, Impact, and Structure Borne Noise," HUD, Washington, D.C., September 1967.)

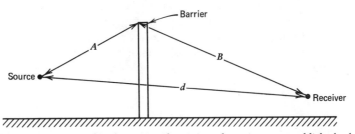

FIGURE 5.5 Geometry for the source, barrier, and receiver to establish the barrier sound attenuation.

in which λ equals the wavelength of the sound in meters. The remaining distances A, B, and d are also measured in meters. Note that we are considering only positive values of N, which means that the receiver is in what is called the shadow zone. Having N, the sound attenuation caused by the barrier, A_b, is obtained from the curve shown in Figure 5.6 for a point source.

Experimental measurements indicate that 24 dB is a practical upper limit for attenuation from such a barrier. If the source and receiver are both

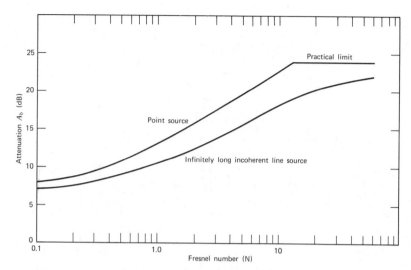

FIGURE 5.6 *Sound attenuation of a solid, straight barrier as a function of the Fresnel number for a point source and an infinitely long incoherent line source.*

close to the barrier, that is, $A + B$ is much larger than d, the curve in Figure 5.6 must be modified to account for strong spherical wave divergence.

Figure 5.6 also shows the attenuation provided by the barrier for an infinitely long incoherent line source parallel to the edge of the barrier. This model has been used in the case of a series of moving sources, such as highway vehicle traffic.

It should be understood that the curves in Figure 5.6 provide only approximate attenuation levels. In the case of outdoor barriers, for example, other factors such as temperature, wind conditions, humidity, atmospheric absorption, and landscaping may be important when estimating the sound attenuation. Further details on these effects can be found in reference 6.

Example 5.3
Referring to Figure 5.5, suppose $A = 20$ m, $B = 35$ m, $d = 50$ m, and the frequency of the point source is 250 Hz. Calculate the attenuation due to the presence of the barrier. For 250 Hz,

$$\lambda = \frac{c}{f} = \frac{344}{250} = 1.376 \text{ m}$$

assuming standard atmospheric conditions. From Equation 5.6,

$$N = \frac{2(20 + 35 - 50)}{1.376} = 7.267$$

Using Figure 5.6 for a point source,

$$A_b = 21.6 \text{ dB} \qquad \text{Answer}$$

5.6 Vibration Isolation

Moving parts of a machine sometimes produce unbalanced forces that are transmitted to the foundation to which the machine is attached. The moving parts generate noise, while the transmitted forces cause movement of the floor that could lead to a structural fatigue problem. A common method of reducing the vibrations transmitted to the foundation utilizes an elastic suspension between the machine and its supporting structure. The elastic suspension has the effect of providing an "impedance mismatch" between the vibrating body and the supporting structure. By this we mean that a material of low acoustic impedance is introduced between materials of high impedance (the machine and its foundation). Materials with a low acoustic impedance lack the ability to transmit energy as fast as materials with high impedance. Materials such as springs, cork, and elastomers, are frequently used alone or in some combination as the elastic suspension for vibration isolation.

Figure 5.7 shows a simple model of an elastically suspended machine represented by a block of weight W and an elastic spring whose stiffness is shown as k. The unbalanced force that produces the vibration is represented by $F \cos \omega t$. The units of each term are:

W = machine weight in newtons
k = spring stiffness in newtons per meter
F = force amplitude in newtons
ω = driving frequency of the force in radians per second
t = time in seconds

The ratio of the force transmitted to the supporting structure to the disturbing force is called the transmissibility, T.R., which is a measure of the amount of isolation present. It can be shown[7] that

$$\text{T.R.} = \frac{\text{force transmitted}}{\text{disturbing force}} = \frac{1}{1 - (\omega/\omega_n)^2} \tag{5.7}$$

in which $\omega_n = \sqrt{kg/W}$, which is called the circular natural frequency of the weight and spring combination. Recall from Chapter 1 that g is the gravitational constant equal to 9.81 m/s^2.

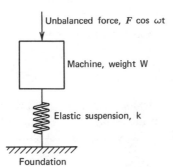

FIGURE 5.7 *Elastic suspension system of an unbalanced machine modeled by a weight and a spring.*

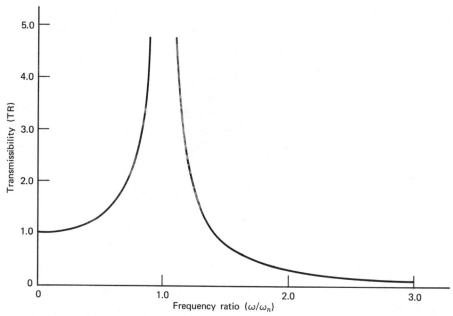

FIGURE 5.8   *Transmissibility of an elastic suspension system as a function of the frequency ration ω/ω_n.*

Figure 5.8 is a plot of the absolute value of the transmissibility as a function of the frequency ratio ω/ω_n. There are three regions to observe in this figure. For low-frequency ratios the transmissibility is close to unity. This means that the machine is supported on a relatively stiff elastic suspension. As the frequency ratio approaches unity, the transmissibility grows significantly. This is the region of resonance in which the driving frequency ω is approximately equal to the natural frequency ω_n. Needless to say, this condition should be avoided to maintain the integrity of the system.

The third region of interest occurs at frequency ratios greater than $\sqrt{2}$. It is in this region that the elastic system consists of a relatively soft spring so that the transmissibility is below a value of unity. Note that the equation for this portion of the curve is $1/[(\omega/\omega_n)^2 - 1]$ since positive values are plotted in the figure. Usually the elastic system is designed to provide a transmissibility of approximately 0.05 to 0.20.

Example 5.4
A motor weighing 70 N runs at 1200 rpm. A transmissibility of 0.15 is desired when the motor is mounted on an elastic spring. What is the spring stiffness k and calculate the natural frequency of the system in revolutions per minute?

Since the desired value of transmissibility is less than unity, we are beyond the region of resonance. The equation for the transmissibility is

$$\text{T.R.} = \frac{1}{(\omega/\omega_n)^2 - 1}$$

We may use the units of revolutions per minute in both the numerator and denominator of ω/ω_n, since we are dealing with the frequency ratio. Consequently, letting the natural frequency be represented by N in units of revolutions per minute, it follows that

$$0.15 = \frac{1}{(1200/N)^2 - 1}$$

$$0.15\left(\frac{1200}{N}\right)^2 = 1.15$$

$$\frac{1200}{N} = 2.77$$

$$N = 433 \text{ rpm} \qquad \text{Answer}$$

Knowing the natural frequency in revolutions per minute, we convert to the circular natural frequency ω_n before calculating the spring stiffness.

$$\omega_n = 433 \text{ rpm} \times \frac{2\pi \text{ rad}}{\text{rev}} \times \frac{\text{min}}{60 \text{ s}} = 45.3 \text{ rad/s}$$

The spring stiffness is now found to be

$$\omega_n = \sqrt{\frac{kg}{W}}$$

Rearranging terms,

$$k = W\frac{\omega_n^2}{g} = \frac{70(45.3)^2}{9.81}$$

$$= 14,600 \frac{\text{N}}{\text{m}} \qquad \text{Answer}$$

5.7 Examples of Noise Control

Sometimes it is necessary to completely enclose a noisy machine. Figure 5.9 indicates the noise reduction achieved for a series of noise control configurations leading to complete enclosure. Figure 5.9a shows the microphone M located to the right of the machine along with the measured octave band levels. Figure 5.9b shows that some reduction occurs in the low-frequency range when vibration isolation mounts are used. The remaining figures are self-explanatory. We see that in Figure 5.9g, the machine, mounted on

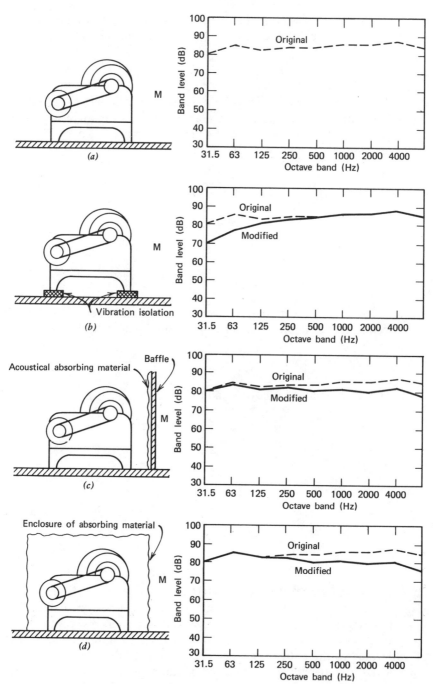

FIGURE 5.9 *Example of noise reduction techniques for a machine.* (*Source. A. P. G. Peterson and E. E. Gross, Jr., Handbook of Noise Measurement, seventh edition, General Radio Co., 1974. Copyright © 1974 by General Radio Co., Concord, Mass.*)

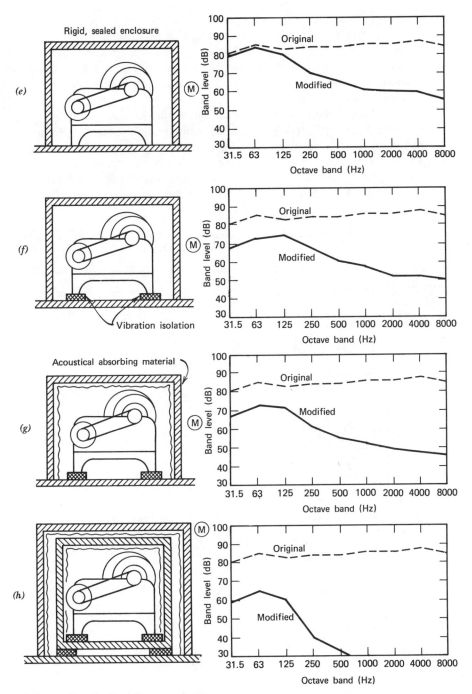

FIGURE 5.9 (Continued)

vibration mounts, is completely enclosed with acoustical absorbing material on the interior of a rigid, sealed enclosure. This arrangement provides rather good noise reduction, which is further improved by a double enclosure, as shown in Figure 5.9*h*. Naturally, the arrangement one selects will depend on the desired noise reduction as well as technological and economic considerations.

Figure 5.10 shows a series of configurations to attenuate noise from a four-lane highway. The L_{10}, which represents the noise level exceeded 10% of the time, is the level used in this figure and is discussed more fully in Chapter 9. For our purposes here, we note that at the right-of-way the noise level is 76 dBA with no barrier. This level decreases to 71 dBA for landscaping 30.5 m thick. The 1.8 m high and 3.7 m high barriers provide reductions to 64

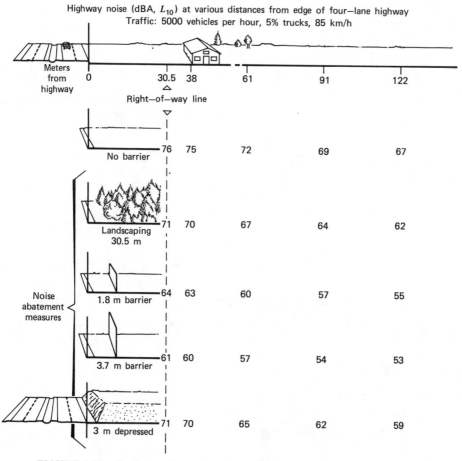

FIGURE 5.10 Outdoor noise attenuation adjacent to a highway by noise reduction techniques. (Source. Dept. of Transportation, FHWA-EIS-72-02-F, November 1972.)

dBA and 61 dBA, respectively. If the highway is depressed 3 m, the level rises to 71 dBA. For each case we observe that the levels naturally decrease as we proceed away from the highway. One note is in order concerning the noise attenuation from landscaping. It can be stated that, generally, landscaping is not a particularly good noise barrier. However, it does serve a good psychological purpose, since the landscaping blocks the sight of the roadway and is aesthetically pleasing to the eye. Consequently, a noise problem might be solved for reasons other than actual noise attenuation.

5.8 Summary

A. The important ideas:
1. Sound control may be viewed as a source-path-receiver systems problem, incorporating economics in arriving at the optimum solution.
2. The reverberation time, an important acoustic property for hearing indoor sounds, is proportional to the room volume and inversely proportional to the room absorption.
3. Both the sound absorption coefficient and the sound transmission loss for materials vary with frequency and are determined under strict measurement conditions.
4. The STC is widely used in evaluating the sound transmission properties of walls, floors, doors, and so forth against sounds of speech, radio, television, and music.
5. Effective noise reduction can be achieved with barriers provided the receiver is in the shadow zone.
6. Elastic suspension of an unbalanced machine can effectively reduce transmitted vibrations to supporting foundations so that structural fatigue and noise are reduced appreciably.

B. The important equations:

1. $T = 0.161 \dfrac{V}{a}$ (5.1)

2. $a = \sum_i \alpha_i S_i$ (5.2)

3. $\text{NR} = 10 \log \left(\dfrac{a_o + a_a}{a_o} \right)$ (5.3)

4. $\text{STL} = L_1 - L_2 + 10 \log \left(\dfrac{S}{a} \right)$ (5.4)

5. $\text{STL} = 20 \log wf - 47.4$ (5.5)

6. $N = \dfrac{2(A + B - d)}{\lambda}$ (5.6)

7. $\text{T.R.} = \dfrac{1}{1 - (\omega/\omega_n)^2}$ (5.7)

5.9 Assignments

5.1 Define reverberation time, sound absorption coefficient, and noise reduction coefficient.

5.2 Calculate the reverberation time for a room 15 m long, 10 m wide, and 4 m high with the following Sabine sound absorption coefficients: ceiling = 0.15; walls = 0.10; floor = 0.06.

5.3 It is decided to use acoustic tile on the ceiling of the room described in problem 5.2. If the Sabine sound absorption coefficient for the ceiling is now 0.55, calculate the reverberation time and the noise reduction.

5.4 A hall 18 m long, 12 m wide, and 5 m high contains an audience of 50 seated adults. The Sabine sound absorption coefficients for the room materials are: ceiling = 0.20; walls = 0.15; floor = 0.12.
Assuming 0.5 sabins per adult, calculate the reverberation time.

5.5 A reverberation room 3 m by 3 m by 3 m is used to establish the Sabine sound absorption coefficients for acoustic materials. The reverberation time of the room is 3.5 s. (a) What is the Sabine sound absorption coefficient of the chamber surfaces? (b) When 5 m² of floor area in the reverberation room is covered with an acoustic material, the reverberation time is 1.2 s. What is the Sabine sound absorption coefficient of this acoustic material?

5.6 Set up a bell as a sound source in the laboratory. Design an enclosure made out of a large sheet of cardboard only (you may use tape and staples for assembling purposes). Measure the sound pressure level reduction on the A-weighting network due to the enclosure at a distance of 2 m from the bell. Limit the weight of your enclosure to 3 N.

5.7 If the sound intensity level incident on a panel is 140 dB, while the radiated sound intensity level from the transmitting side is 85 dB, what is the STL?

5.8 For what types of noise should the STC ratings be used?

5.9 What restrictions were made in this chapter on the development of sound attenuation by barriers against outdoor noise?

5.10 A sound source with a frequency of 300 Hz is to be attenuated by a barrier. Referring to Figure 5.5, what is the attenuation if $A = 15$ m, $B = 22$ m, and $d = 32$ m?

5.11 Figure 5.11 shows a source and receiver at the same height above the

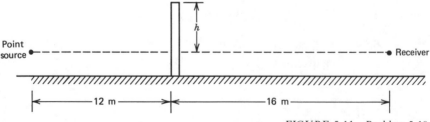

FIGURE 5.11   Problem 5.10.

ground. If an attenuation of 15 dB is specified, find h for the wall, assuming the source frequency is 800 Hz.

5.12 Repeat problem 5.11 if the source frequency equals 400 Hz.

5.13 What is the maximum value of the height H for the receiver shown in Figure 5.12 to remain in the shadow zone?

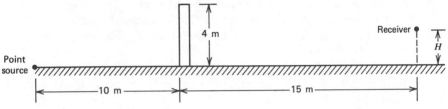

FIGURE 5.12   Problem 5.13.

5.14 A motor weighing 55 N is mounted on an elastic suspension whose stiffness equals 10,000 N/m. Find the natural frequency of the system and express it in Hertz.

5.15 Find the stiffness k of an elastic suspension for an unbalanced machine weighing 80 N and running at 1000 rpm if the design transmissibility equals 0.20.

5.16 In a vibration test of a block mounted on a spring, a resonance of 500 Hz is measured. If the block weighs 10 N, what is the elastic stiffness k of the spring?

5.17 Calculate the sound transmission loss provided by a partition 3 m by 4 m if the time average sound pressure levels in the source room and receiving room are 90 dB and 72 dB, respectively. Assume the sound absorption of the receiving room is 20 sabins.

5.18 Calculate the sound transmission loss of gypsum wall board 25.4 mm thick and whose area density equals 16.5 kg/m^2 if the sound frequency equals (a) 500 Hz, and (b) 1000 Hz.

5.19 A wall is to provide a sound transmission loss of 45 dB. If the sound frequency is 1000 Hz, what is the required area density of the material?

5.20 A partition is inserted between two rooms in which the time space average sound pressure level equals 85 dB in the source room and 60 dB in the receiving room. If the total radiating surface area of the partition equals 35 m^2 and the total sound absorption in the receiving room equals 50 sabins, calculate the sound transmission loss.

5.21 A room 16 m long, 12 m wide, and 4 m high has the following Sabine sound absorption coefficients:

Ceiling $= 0.10$ Walls $= 0.18$ Floor $= 0.05$

What is the required absorption coefficient of floor carpeting to achieve a noise reduction of 5 dB?

References

[1] *Sound Control Construction*, second edition, U.S. Gypsum, 1972.

[2] L. F. Yerges, *Sound, Noise, and Vibration Control*, Van Nostrand Reinhold, 1969.

[3] L. E. Kinsler and A. R. Frey, *Fundamentals of Acoustics*, second edition, John Wiley, 1962.

[4] L. L. Beranek, *Noise and Vibration Control*, Chapter 11, McGraw-Hill, 1971.

[5] ASTM E 90-70, "Recommended Practice for Laboratory Measurement of Airborne Sound Transmission Loss of Building Partitions," American Society for Testing and Materials, Philadelphia.

[6] L. L. Beranek, *Noise and Vibration Control*, Chapter 7, McGraw-Hill, 1971.

[7] C. R. Freberg and E. N. Kemler, *Elements of Mechanical Vibration*, second edition, John Wiley, 1949.

6

SPEECH AND HEARING

Speech and hearing are two vital senses that enable us to communicate with each other. While we are principally concerned with hearing effects from environmental noise pollution in this text, the subject of speech is introduced, since it is a primary sound source in our lives. Our hearing ability is something we take for granted. However, its acuity can be dulled and destroyed by abuse when we place ourselves in environments where the sound intensity is loud enough and the time exposure is long enough to cause damage.

In this chapter we study the voice mechanism, the ear anatomy, and how we hear. Our hearing characteristics are examined, including the distinction between loudness level and apparent loudness. Finally, we begin our treatment of hearing loss by introducing the subject of audiometry and some current theories on hearing damage.

6.1 Speech

When speaking, our chest muscles force air from our lungs upward by contraction. This effort supplies a steady air stream, which forms the sound energy for speech. The pressure and velocity of the air stream are modulated, which allows us to express voiced and unvoiced sounds. The larynx, located next to the thyroid cartilage (Adam's apple), is the primary modulating agent for voiced sounds. The vocal chords consist of two membranelike elastic tissues stretched across the larynx and controlled by small muscles attached to the glottis wall. These muscles control the tension, shape, and spacing of the vocal chords, which affect the frequency of the voiced sounds. Further modification of the pressure occurs in the air flowing through the many resonating cavities and orifices of the throat, nose, and mouth. Finally, additional control is obtained by our tongue, teeth, and lip formation. In the case of unvoiced sounds, such as the forcible exhaling of air, the vocal chords are not used.

To give us an idea of the wide range of sound power associated with speech, consider the following average values.

Shouting: 10^{-3} W

Conversational speech: 10^{-5} W

Whispering: 10^{-9} W

The frequencies of speech range from 200 to 10,000 Hz, while the frequency range between 1000 to 2500 Hz is required for speech intelligibility. In fact, telephones transmit speech between 250 to 2750 Hz, which allows us to recognize who is speaking in addition to what is being said.

6.2 The Ear Anatomy

The ear is a remarkable organ capable of performing wide-ranging feats. For example, our ears hear sound pressures as low as 2×10^{-5} Pa to as high as 200 Pa before experiencing pain. The audible frequency response for a very good ear ranges from approximately 16 to 20,000 Hz. Sounds below 16 Hz are called infrasound, while those above 20,000 Hz are called ultrasound.

Figure 6.1 illustrates the main parts of the ear, while Figure 6.2 is a schematic representation of the ear in which the cochlea, a small snailshaped body, is purposely straightened out for convenience. The three main divisions of the ear are:

1. Outer ear

   Pinna. The outside agent, which serves as a horn.

   Auditory canal. Approximately a straight tube, 7 mm in diameter, 25 mm long.

   Eardrum. A membrane stretched across the end of the auditory canal. The eardrum is also called the tympanic membrane.

2. Middle ear. This is an air-filled chamber.

   Ossicles. The name of the chain of three tiny bones called the malleous (hammer), incus (anvil), and stapes (stirrup). These bones transmit the vibrations of the tympanic membrane to the oval window.

   Eustachian tube. Establishes equilibrium between the outside air pressure and the pressure in the middle ear.

3. Inner ear. Contains the perilymph liquid in the cavity containing the membranes and nerve endings by which sound energy changes are detected, analyzed, and transmitted to the auditory nerves.

   Vestibule. The entrance chamber.

   Semicircular canals. Provide for our sense of balance.

   Cochlea. Contains the organ of Corti, which is the sense organ for hearing. Figure 6.3 shows a cross section of the cochlea,

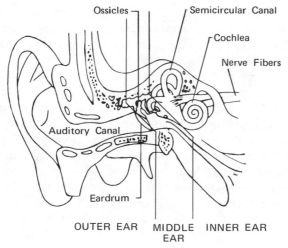

FIGURE 6.1   Cross-section of the ear. (*Source. J. T. Broch, Acoustic Noise Measurements, B & K Instruments, Inc. January 1971.*)

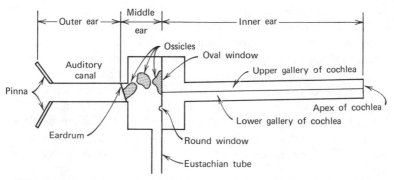

FIGURE 6.2   Schematic drawing of the ear with the cochlea straightened out for identification purposes.

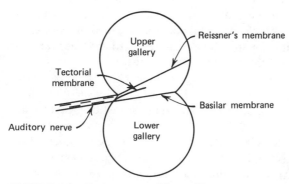

FIGURE 6.3   Cross section of the cochlea.

which includes Reissner's membrane, the tectorial membrane, and the basilar membrane. There are approximately 23,500 minute hair cells embedded between the basilar membrane and the tectorial membrane distributed along the organ of Corti. The terminal endings of the nerve fibers shown in Figure 6.3 are also embedded in these hair cells. The cochlea is divided primarily by the basilar membrane into the upper gallery and the lower gallery, as indicated in Figure 6.2. The basilar membrane is relatively stiff near the oval window and gradually increases in mass while decreasing in stiffness along the cochlea toward the apex. This description of the cochlea was made by Georg von Bekesy in the 1930s and 1940s. For this and other discoveries, he received a Nobel prize in 1961.

6.3 How We Hear

When sound waves impinge on the pinna, they travel down the auditory canal and set the eardrum vibrating. The ossicles transmit these vibrations to the inner ear at the oval window. These vibrations, in turn, generate elastic waves through the perilymph fluid; the waves proceed from the oval window, along the upper gallery, around the apex, and through the lower gallery, terminating at the round window. Because of the variation in mass and stiffness of the basilar membrane, high-frequency waves produce large displacements of the basilar membrane near the oval window, while low-frequency waves produce large displacements of the basilar membrane near the apex. The cochlea, in effect, acts very much like a frequency analyzer, so that our hearing enables us to discriminate between tones of different frequency.

The displacement of the basilar membrane produces a bending effect on the hair cells embedded between the tectorial membrane and the basilar membrane. The straining of these hair cells generate electrical pulses (a piezoelectric effect) through the auditory nerve endings and ultimately to the brain. This measureable electrical potential is called the *cochlea potential*. Other routes available for sound waves to travel to the inner ear include the skull bones or holes in the eardrum, if they exist.

We do have the ability to protect our inner ear from intense noise levels using the two smallest muscles in the body, the tensor tympani and the stapedius. This action on our part is called the acoustic reflex, by which these muscles in the middle ear enable us to stiffen the eardrum membrane and the movement of the ossicles. Unfortunately, this reflex action takes place within a few hundreds of a second after a sound reaches the outer ear. Consequently, in the case of unexpected high-impact noise, severe damage might occur before the acoustic reflex is implemented. A warning sound of moderate intensity preceding such noise would allow us to apply the acoustic reflex to advantage.

Another interesting feature of our hearing is that the ear behaves non-linearly. For example, if two pure tones, each in the audible range of high intensity, differ in frequency by an amount that is also in the audible range, we may hear a distinct difference tone that corresponds to this difference frequency. Because of the nonlinear characteristics of our hearing, we can also listen to a single tone of high intensity and may hear an aural harmonic whose frequency is a multiple of the original tone frequency. Whether we hear the difference tones and aural harmonics will depend largely on the test conditions and our hearing acuity.

6.4 Loudness and Loudness Level

Psychoacoustics data have been obtained on the human perception to pure tones. Generally, the data are obtained by alternately listening to a reference tone at 1000 Hz and, after an elapsed time interval, a second tone at some other frequency. The person being tested is required to adjust the second tone until the two tones seem to be equally loud. Figure 6.4 shows a set of equal loudness contours that have been internationally standardized. A contour of equal loudness is labeled by the term phon, which is the unit of loudness level of a pure tone equal numerically to the intensity level of a 1000-Hz tone

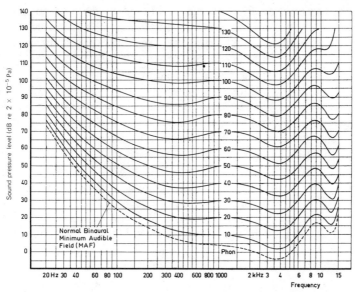

FIGURE 6.4   Internationally standardized set of equal loudness level contours. (Source. J. T. Broch, Acoustic Noise Measurements, B & K Instruments, Inc., January 1971.)

judged to be equally loud. For example, a pure tone of a 100-Hz, 30-dB sound pressure level sounds as loud as a 1000-Hz, 10-dB tone. Both are rated at a loudness level of 10 phons.

In examining the equal loudness level contours in Figure 6.4 we observe that there is a minimum audible curve that forms the threshold of audibility. We also note that the ear requires different levels of sound intensity for different tones to appear equally loud. Starting at 20 Hz, the intensity is relatively high, decreasing as the tone frequency increases. Between 3000 and 4000 Hz, the ear is most sensitive to the tone. Above this frequency range, the intensity required to hear the tone increases once more.

It is precisely this property of our hearing that the weighting networks used with sound level meters are derived. For example, it was mentioned earlier that the A-weighting network was originally adopted to simulate our response to relatively low sound levels, the B-weighting network for moderate sound levels, and the C-weighting network for high sound levels. By inverting selected phon contours, we obtain the A, B, and C weighting curves shown earlier in Figure 4.7.

In addition to the threshold of audibility, there is also a threshold of feeling and a threshold of pain. Both of these thresholds are represented by relatively flat contours across the frequency range of hearing with the threshold of feeling at approximately 120 dB and the threshold of pain ranging between 135 to 140 dB.

Unfortunately, the phon scale for the equal loudness level contours is not applicable as a true loudness scale. In other words, 80 phons does not appear to be twice as loud as 40 phons. We would like to have a true loudness scale such that if we double the units for loudness, we double the subjective loudness. One method to determine such a scale was introduced by Fletcher,[1] an early researcher in psychoacoustics. The theory is that two pure tones of quite different frequencies stimulate different portions of the basilar membrane. Consequently, the subjective response to both tones acting together should be additive. The experiment adds two selected tones of equal loudness level to form a complex sound wave. One of these tones is then adjusted until both the complex sound and the tone seem equally loud. The resulting value for the single tone is therefore twice as loud as either component forming the complex wave. The process can be repeated for several tones forming the complex wave. Up to 10 tones have been used to establish a subjective determination for a loudness ratio of 10 to 1. From the data collected by Fletcher, a relationship between the loudness level in phons and the subjective level in sones has been established, where one sone is defined as the loudness of a 1000 Hz tone of 40 dB intensity. Figure 6.5 shows the results graphically; they are expressed mathematically as

$$S = 2^{(P-40)/10} \qquad\qquad (6.1)$$

in which S is in sones and P is in phons. The results show that the subjective

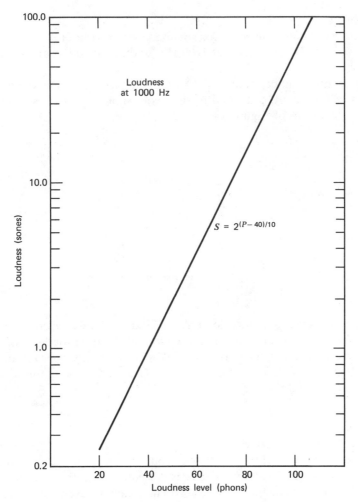

FIGURE 6.5   *Graphical relationship between loudness in sones and loudness level in phons.*

loudness doubles for an increase of 10 phons. An increase of about 1/2 phon corresponds to the minimum perceptable change in loudness.[2]

We are now in a position to predict the loudness from simultaneous exposure to several pure tones widely spaced in frequency and about equally loud. This is achieved by converting the sound pressure level of each tone to phons by means of Figure 6.4. Each phon, in turn, is converted to sones by Equation 6.1 or Figure 6.5. The sones are added arithmetically to establish the total loudness. For a more detailed description of this procedure, refer to reference 3 at the end of this chapter.

Example 6.1

Calculate the loudness in sones for simultaneous exposure to the following tones: 60 dB at 340 Hz, 65 dB at 1600 Hz, 70 dB at 2960 Hz, and 65 dB at 4000 Hz.

The solution is best illustrated in tabular form. The sound pressure levels in column 2 are converted to their corresponding loudness levels in column 3 by means of Figure 6.4.

Frequency (Hz)	Sound Pressure Level (dB)	Loudness Level (phons)	Loudness (sones)
340	60	64	5.3
1600	65	66	6.1
2960	70	78	13.9
4000	65	75	11.3
		Summation =	36.6

Using Figure 6.5 or Equation 6.1, the loudness levels are converted to sones in column 4. From Figure 6.5 we see that the total loudness of 36.6 sones corresponds to a 1000-Hz tone of 92 phons. Finally, we can say that a 1000-Hz tone of 92 dB sounds as loud as the above four tones being generated simultaneously.

6.5 Calculating Loudness

We can extend the loudness effects from pure tones to practical situations in which steady-state, wide-band noise is present, such as the noise from an air conditioner. One method is based on octave band measurements, each of which is converted over to sones by using the family of curves shown in Figure 6.6. These values are added as follows to obtain the equivalent sone value, S_{eq}.

$$S_{eq} = 0.3 \sum_i S_i + 0.7 S_{max} \qquad (6.2)$$

in which S_i = octave band loudness index

$\qquad S_{max}$ = maximum octave band loudness index

Having S_{eq}, the conversion chart in Figure 6.6 is used to find the equivalent phon value.

Expressing the loudness in sones has the advantage that it allows a direct comparison between noise sources. For example, the Home Ventilating Institute certifies equipment in sones, so that if one ventilating system is rated 8 sones and another 4 sones, then one is twice as loud as the other.

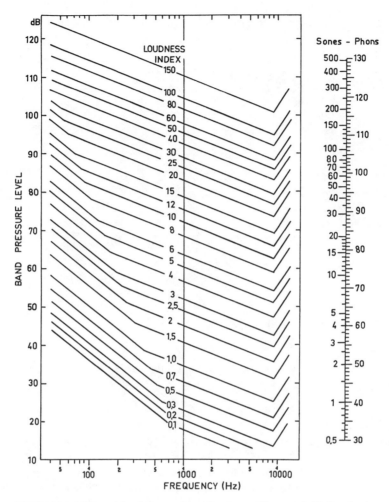

FIGURE 6.6   *Equal loudness contours in sones.* (*Source. J. T. Broch, Acoustic Noise Measurements, B & K Instruments, Inc., January 1971.*)

It must be emphasized that the above method is applicable to sound spectra that are relatively smooth in a diffuse sound field. No pure tones may be present to use the method.[4] More complicated situations have been studied by Kryter[5] to take into account both the time duration of the noise level and the spectral complexity. The investigation has lead to what is called the perceived noisiness, which we shall examine in a later chapter.

Example 6.2
Calculate the loudness in phons for the following octave band data.

The table below summarizes the calculations with the aid of Figure 6.6.

Frequency (Hz)	i	Sound Pressure Level L_i (dB)	Octave Band Loudness Index, S_i
63	1	55	1.1
125	2	65	3.7
250	3	66	5.0
500	4	63.5	5.3
1000	5	65	6.5
2000	6	59.5	5.6
4000	7	51	4.0
8000	8	45	3.4
			$\sum_i S_i = \overline{34.6}$

Substituting into Equation 6.2,

$$S_{eq} = 0.3(34.6) + 0.7(6.5)$$
$$= 14.9 \text{ sones}$$

From the conversion chart in Figure 6.6, this corresponds to 79 phons.

6.6 Audiometry

An audiometer is an instrument that measures our hearing acuity. Discrete pure tones, usually at 250, 500, 1000, 2000, 3000, 4000, 6000, and 8000 Hz, are used to establish our auditory threshold. These auditory levels are referenced to zero values at each frequency, which have been set by international agreement. An audiometer should conform to a standard such as the ISO/R-389-1964 and the test should be conducted in a quiet surrounding.

Figure 6.7 shows the results of two audiograms of an 18-year-old man who experienced several hours of relatively high noise levels in a power plant. The curve labeled preexposure is the man's permanent hearing threshold measured before entering the plant. Shortly after leaving the plant, another audiogram was taken and is labeled postexposure. We observe that a hearing loss occurred because of the noise exposure. This is an example of a noise-induced temporary threshold shift (NITTS), since the ear did recover the hearing loss shortly thereafter. By definition, a NITTS recovers within a few seconds up to a few days. A noise-induced permanent threshold shift (NIPTS) usually shows no recovery after two to three weeks.[6]

We now examine currently held hearing damage theories that are based on industrial noise data for workers exposed to steady noise.

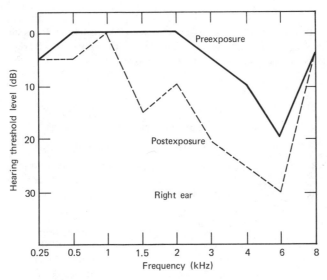

FIGURE 6.7   Example of a noise induced temporary threshold shift experienced by an 18-year old after several hours in a power plant.

1. *The equal temporary effect theory* states that the long-term hazard of a NIPTS of steady-state noise exposure is predicted by the average NITTS produced by the same daily noise in the healthy young ear. Those steady noise levels that produce NITTS in young people will ultimately produce NIPTS. This theory does indicate that intermittant noise exposure is much less harmful than unbroken exposure to steady-state noise at the same level. Allowing a factory worker periodic relief from the steady din may be an effective measure in hearing conservation.

2. *The equal-energy theory* argues that the hazard to one's hearing is determined by the total amount of sound energy entering the ear on a daily basis. It follows that an 8-h exposure to 85 dB is equivalent in acoustic energy exposure as 4 h at 88 dB. That is, as we increase the energy exposure by 3 dB, the time exposure is cut in half for the sound energy to be equivalent. Wearing a noise dosimeter, which measures cumulative noise exposure, would provide useful data to evaluate a factory worker's potential to hearing damage under this theory.

6.7 **Hearing Conservation Criteria**

There is a difference of opinion as to what constitutes normal hearing.[7] Some say normal hearing is the ability to detect sounds between 16 to 20,000 Hz at levels that lie at or within 10 dB of the normal threshold of hearing

TABLE 6.1

Guideline for the Relations Between the Average Hearing Threshold Level for 500, 1000, and 2000 Hz and Degree of Handicap as Defined by the Committee on Hearing of the American Academy of Ophthalmology and Otolaryngology.

Class	Degree of Handicap	Average Hearing Threshold Level for 500, 1000, and 2000 Hz in the Better Ear		Ability To Understand Speech
		More Than (dB)	Not More Than (dB)	
A	Not significant		25	No significant difficulty with faint speech
B	Slight handicap	25	40	Difficulty only with faint speech
C	Mild handicap	40	55	Frequent difficulty with normal speech
D	Marked handicap	55	70	Frequent difficulty with loud speech
E	Severe handicap	70	90	Can understand only shouted or amplified speech
F	Extreme handicap	90		Usually cannot understand amplified speech

Source. Davis, 1965, Transactions of the American Academy of Ophthalmology and Otolaryngology.

and below the threshold of aural pain in human beings. Many otologists define normal hearing as the ability to respond appropriately to human speech in average daily situations, so that the frequency range of interest lies between 250 and 4000 Hz. An example of this viewpoint is seen in Table 6.1, in which different classes of hearing handicaps are listed based on average hearing threshold levels for tones at 500, 1000, and 2000 Hz in the better ear. Here we observe that an average hearing threshold level greater than 25 dB in the better ear is considered a handicap of some degree.

The U.S. Environmental Protection Agency (EPA) recently adopted[8] a hearing conservation criteria designed to protect the public health and welfare with an adequate margin of safety. The EPA examined steady noise levels occurring 8 h a day, 5 days a week, over a period of 40 yr, and their resulting effect on the population so as to cause a 5 dB NIPTS at 4000 Hz. This frequency of 4000 Hz was chosen, since hearing damage from noise generally develops first at this sensitive auditory frequency. Figure 6.8 shows the curve developed by EPA from these extensive research results; it relates the percentage of exposed population that will incur no more than 5 dB NIPTS as a function of exposure level. EPA selected 73 dBA from this curve,

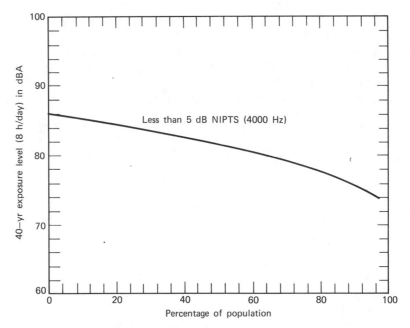

FIGURE 6.8   Percentage of exposed population that will incur no more than 5 dB NIPTS shown as a function of exposed level. Population ranked by decreasing ability to hear at 4000 Hz. (Source. "Information on Levels of Environmental Noise Requisite to Protect Public Health and Welfare with an Adequate Margin of Safety," EPA, March 1974.)

which corresponds to 96 percent of the population being protected. This level was modified to account for the fact that most environmental noise is intermittant, not continuous. Another correction accounted for a yearly dose of 365 days compared to 250 working days for which Figure 6.8 is based on; finally, a correction was made to adjust from an 8-h day in Figure 6.8 to a 24-h day. These corrections lead to 70 dBA as the recommended yearly average equivalent sound level to protect the public health from hearing damage caused by environmental noise pollution.

6.8 Summary

A. The important ideas:

1. The larynx is the primary modulating agent for voiced sounds.
2. The cochlea potential represents the electrical pulses sent through the nerve endings in the organ of Corti to the brain when the microscopic hair cells are strained due to the basilar membrane motion.

3. Loudness level is expressed in phons, while the apparent loudness is expressed in sones.
4. Because our hearing requires different intensity levels to hear sounds at different frequencies, weighting networks have been incorporated into sound level meters.
5. We may experience a temporary threshold shift in hearing if the noise exposure is loud enough and long enough.
6. EPA has selected a 24-h exposure of 70 dBA as the level that will protect the average individual from hearing damage caused by environmental noise pollution occurring over many years.

B. The important equations:

1. $S = 2^{(P-40)/10}$ (6.1)

2. $S_{eq} = 0.3 \sum_i S_i + 0.7 S_{max}$ (6.2)

6.9 Assignments

6.1 Distinguish between the frequency speech range, the frequency range for normal hearing, and the frequency range required for speech intelligibility.

6.2 Explain the role of the vocal chords in forming voiced sounds.

6.3 List the three parts of the outer ear and explain the function of each.

6.4 What parts are contained in the middle ear and what is the function of each?

6.5 Make a sketch of the inner ear and label each major part.

6.6 Why is the ear capable of distinguishing between tones of different frequencies?

6.7 What is meant by the cochlea potential?

6.8 What is (a) a difference tone, (b) an aural harmonic?

6.9 Distinguish between the loudness level in phons and the loudness in sones.

6.10 At what level does (a) the threshold of feeling occur, (b) the threshold of pain occur?

6.11 Find the loudness level for the following pure tones: (a) 50 dB at 100 Hz; (b) 50 dB at 4000 Hz.

6.12 Find the loudness level for the following pure tones: (a) 70 dB at 500 Hz; (b) 100 dB at 500 Hz.

6.13 Find the loudness level and loudness for a pure tone of 60 dB at 250 Hz. What must the intensity level be for this tone to decrease its loudness 20%?

6.14 Which of the following four tones is loudest? (a) 90 dB at 30 Hz; (b) 90 dB at 400 Hz; (c) 90 dB at 3500 Hz; or (d) 90 dB at 8000 Hz.

6.15 Calculate the loudness in sones for simultaneous exposure to the following pure tones: 72 dB at 200 Hz; 84 dB at 2500 Hz; 90 dB at 6000 Hz. At what level is a 1000 Hz tone equivalent to the calculated loudness?

6.16 Calculate the loudness in sones for simultaneous exposure to the following pure tones: 95 dB at 250 Hz; 85 dB at 700 Hz; 70 dB at 2000 Hz. At what level is a 1000 Hz tone equivalent to the calculated loudness?

6.17 Calculate the equivalent sone value and phon value for the following octave band data taken inside a small aircraft.

f_c (Hz)	Octave Band Sound Pressure Level (dB)
63	95
125	88
250	76
500	82
1000	85
2000	75
4000	60
8000	50

6.18 (a) Calculate the overall dBA level for the octave band data shown in Figure 6.9. (b) Calculate the equivalent sone value and phon value.

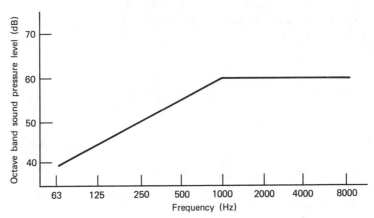

FIGURE 6.9   Problem 6.18.

6.19 (a) Calculate the overall dBA level for the octave band data shown in Figure 6.10. (b) Calculate the equivalent sone value and phon value.

6.20 Set up two oscillators to a speaker system so that you can hear two tones simultaneously. Select two tones of the same intensity but whose

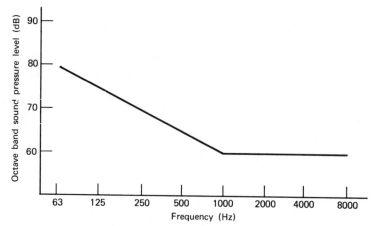

FIGURE 6.10   Problem 6.19.

frequencies differ by 2 Hz. Listen to what is called the *beat* phenomenon, a sound characteristic used for tuning musical instruments.

6.21 Using the setup in problem 6.20, try to identify an aural harmonic of a tone of 400 Hz. Use the beat phenomenon to assist you in identifying the aural harmonic at 800 Hz by generating a tone at 802 Hz while listening to the 400-Hz tone.

6.22 Distinguish between the noise-induced temporary threshold shift and the noise-induced permanent threshold shift.

6.23 Explain the two hearing damage theories for long-term exposure to steady noise.

References

[1] H. Fletcher, "Loudness, Masking and Their Relation to the Hearing Process and the Problem of Noise Measurement," *J. Acoust. Soc. Am.*, Vol. 9, p. 275, 1938.

[2] L. E. Kinsler and A. R. Frey, *Fundamentals of Acoustics*, second edition, Chapter 13, John Wiley, 1962.

[3] L. L. Beranek, *Acoustics*, Chapter 13, McGraw Hill, 1954.

[4] J. T. Broch, *Acoustic Noise Measurements*, Bruel & Kjaer, January 1971.

[5] K. Kryter, *Effects of Noise on Man*, Academic Press, 1970.

[6] L. L. Beranek, *Noise and Vibration Control*, Chapter 17, McGraw-Hill, 1971.

[7] "Public Health and Welfare Criteria for Noise," U.S. Environmental Protection Agency, Section 4, July 27 1973.

[8] "Information on Levels of Environmental Noise Requisite to Protect Public Health and Welfare with an Adequate Margin of Safety," U.S. Environmental Protection Agency, March 1974.

7
EFFECTS OF NOISE ON PEOPLE

Today's environment exposes each of us to noise levels that may be damaging to our hearing, may produce interference with the activities in our daily lives, and may degrade the quality of our life-style. Noise effects are no longer studied simply as an occupational health problem in which a workman's hearing is damaged due to long-term exposure on the job. Instead, it encompasses all noise for both indoor and outdoor environments occupied by living beings.

This chapter introduces us to some important topics normally treated in the general areas of physiological acoustics and psychoacoustics. These include an overview of the effects from excessive noise exposure on our hearing, speech communication, sleep, degree of annoyance, and other undesirable by-products of noise pollution. We shall see that noise affects us in many ways, ranging from physiological effects to psychological effects.

7.1 Auditory Effects

When we are exposed to intense noise levels, some or all of the hair cells in the organ of Corti may be damaged temporarily or permanently. Temporary damage means that our hearing threshold level has shifted temporarily due to the noise exposure. Given adequate time for recovery in quieter surroundings, our hearing threshold returns to its original threshold level. Thus, a noise induced temporary threshold shift (NITTS) occurs. Examples of threshold shifts between preexposure and postexposure are shown in Figures 7.1 to 7.3 for nonoccupational environments. In each case the postexposure audiogram was taken after the individual left the noise environment, but as soon as practical thereafter.

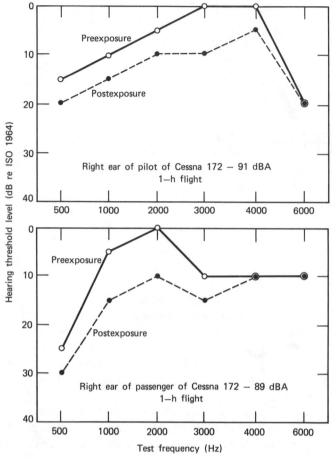

FIGURE 7.1 *Hearing threshold level shifts in the right ear of a pilot and a passenger after a 91 dBA exposure level in a Cessna 172 airplane. (Source. A. Cohen, J. Anticaglia, and H. H. Jones, "Sociocusis-Hearing Loss from Non-Occupational Noise Exposure," Sound & Vibration, November 1970.)*

In most cases of hearing loss, there is a gradual shifting of the threshold of hearing due to repeated exposure to noise, such as a factory worker exposed to high noise levels over a span of several years. This is called noise-induced cochlea injury. There is a gradual deterioration of the cells in the organ of Corti due to excessive overexposure to noise. Some believe that the cells must work at a metabolic rate so high that the cells simply die from fatigue. For example, if the musicians in Figure 7.3 play several times a week, their noise induced temporary threshold shift becomes chronic. Such chronically maintained postexposure changes may loose their temporary quality and become permanent, leading to a permanent threshold shift.

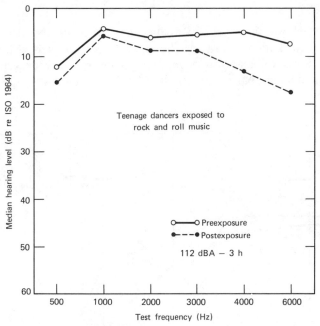

FIGURE 7.2 *Median hearing threshold level shifts for teenage dancers exposed to rock and roll music, 112 dBA for 3 h. (Source. A. Cohen, J. Anticaglia, and H. H. Jones, "Sociocusis-Hearing Loss from Non-Occupational Noise Exposure," Sound & Vibration, November 1970.)*

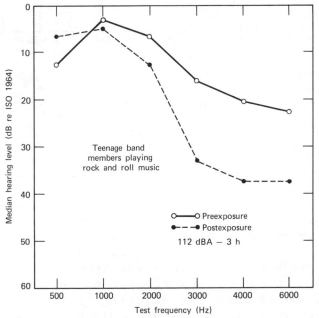

FIGURE 7.3 *Median hearing threshold level shifts for teenage band members playing rock and roll music, 112 dBA for 3 h. (Source. A. Cohen, J. Anticaglia, and H. H. Jones, "Sociocusis-Hearing Loss from Non-Occupational Noise Exposure," Sound & Vibration, November 1970.)*

Figure 7.4 shows the results of a study into permanent hearing loss among women working in a weaving shop over various periods of time. It is clear that those women with longer time exposures have experienced greater hearing damage, particularly in the 4000-Hz region.

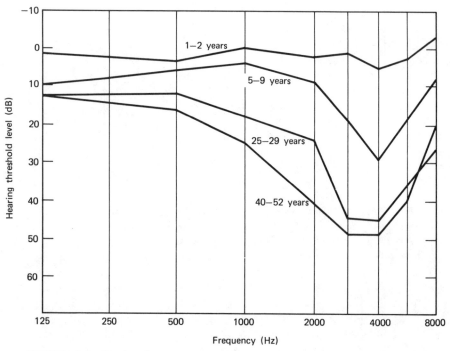

FIGURE 7.4   Results of an investigation into the permanent hearing loss among women working in a weaving shop over periods of time. (Source. W. Taylor, J. Pearson, A. Mair, and W. Burns, "Study of Noise and Hearing in Jute Weaving," J. Ac. Soc. Am., Vol. 38, 1965.)

Presbycusis is the term that describes the loss of auditory sensitivity with increasing age, independent of occupational noise exposure. This is characterized by older people who have difficulty understanding speech. The process is a result of changes in the inner ear with age along with other effects caused by disease, toxic drugs, and nonoccupational noise exposure. Figure 7.5 shows the average shifts with age of the thresholds of hearing for pure tones for men and women. In 1962, a study was conducted on the hearing of members of the Mabaan tribe, who are located in a remote part of the Sudan. Their hearing was judged to be far superior to people who are exposed to noise levels found in industrialized nations. This is demonstrated by

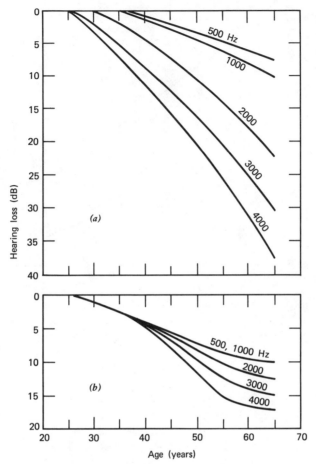

FIGURE 7.5 *Shift in average threshold of hearing with age as a function of frequency.*
(a) Men (b) Women. (Source. "The Relations of Hearing Loss to Noise Exposure,"
ASA Subcommittee Z24-X-2, 1954.)

Figure 7.6, which compares the hearing loss with age for members of the Mabaan tribe with Americans who are divided between those who work in noise-related industry and those who do not.[1] We observe that at age 60, the average hearing loss for the Mabaan tribe reaches 10 dB, for the nonnoise-exposed Americans between 10 and 38 dB, and for the noise-exposed Americans between 38 and 62 dB.

A noise-induced permanent threshold shift (NIPTS) can occur from a catastrophic noise exposure such as a firecracker exploding close to one's ear. Figure 7.7 is an example of such a case; it shows the hearing threshold before the accident, 1 week after the accident, and 5 months after the accident. An injury of this type is called an acoustic trauma. When this occurs the

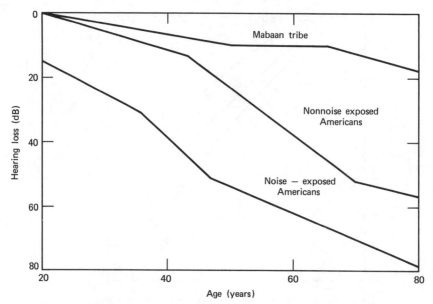

FIGURE 7.6 *Hearing loss as a function of age for the Mabaan tribe, nonnoise-exposed Americans, and noise-exposed Americans. (Source. G. Chedd, Sound, Doubleday, New York, p. 168, 1970.)*

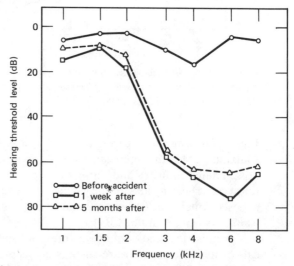

FIGURE 7.7 *Example of acoustic trauma caused by a firecracker exploding close to a person's ear. (Source. A. Cohen, J. Anticaglia, and H. H. Jones, Sociocusis-Hearing Loss from Non-Occupational Noise Exposure," Sound & Vibration, November, 1970.)*

organ of Corti may be torn apart, or the structural damage to the inner ear may be so great that the hair cells soon die from the disruption.

7.2 Speech Interference

We have all experienced the problem of trying to understand another person talking to us in an environment with a high background noise level. We may have difficulty understanding the verbal communication for a number of reasons, such as one's age, speech pronunciation, and our own hearing acuity. For example, children and the elderly will probably experience more difficulty in understanding speech than a person with good hearing in the same situation. The high background noise level provides a masking effect on the sounds that the person is trying to hear.

Measurements have been made on speech interference, and the results are generally characterized by two methods, the articulation index (AI) and the speech interference level (SIL). The latter method was introduced by L. Beranek in 1947 as a simpler approach than the AI method, which is somewhat involved.[2] To establish the SIL, we measure the distance between two persons required for reliable speech communication using unexpected word material under a steady noise level background. The SIL is obtained for a particular voice effort by taking the arithmetic average of the octave band sound pressure levels of the background noise. When originally proposed, the old octave bands were in use so that the arithmetic average was taken in the frequency bands 600 to 1200, 1200 to 2400, and 2400 to 4800 Hz. Today the new octave bands are used so that the average is taken at the center frequencies of 500, 1000, and 2000 Hz. This latter measurement is called the preferred speech interference level (PSIL). It is sometimes written PSIL (0.5, 1, 2), in which the center frequencies are placed in parentheses in kilo-Hertz (kHz).

The data for PSIL are arranged in a way that relate the PSIL with the voice effort and the distance between the speaker and the listener facing each other. The data can be converted from PSIL values to dBA levels to provide a graphical presentation, as shown in Figure 7.8. Note that the data in Figure 7.8 are for the outdoor environment only. For example, if the background noise level is 60 dBA, the speaker and listener must be approximately 0.62 m apart, facing each other, for relaxed conversation (sentence intelligibility = 99 percent). This distance increases to 1.9 m for normal voice effort and to 3.8 m for raised voice effort.

Recommended background noise levels that avoid indoor speech interference problems have been developed in octave band form and are known as the preferred noise criteria (PNC) curves. These curves are shown in Figure 7.9. Depending on the use of the room, we select a PNC curve that we set as the design limit. The background level in each octave band should not exceed the corresponding level on the PNC curve. For example, the

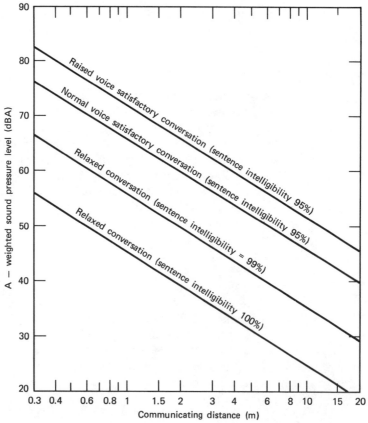

FIGURE 7.8   Maximum distances outdoors over which conversation is considered to be satisfactorily intelligible in steady noise. (Source. "Information on Levels of Environmental Noise Requisite to Protect Public Health and Welfare with an Adequate Margin of Safety," EPA, March 1974.)

background octave band levels plotted in Figure 7.10 indicate that a PNC-45 curve is satisfied. In place of octave band levels, overall A-weighted levels may be more convenient to use for many indoor situations. Recommended indoor levels are shown in Table 7.1 for a wide variety of situations.

Speech interference is usually one of the human effects from environmental noise pollution taken into consideration when setting noise standards or regulations. For example, in addition to the hearing conservation level adopted by EPA that was described in Chapter 6, speech interference was examined as an important basis for evaluating activity interference from environmental noise. Both indoor and outdoor situations were examined by EPA, as we shall see in a later chapter.

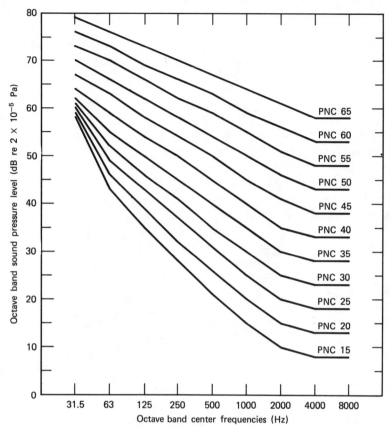

FIGURE 7.9 Recommended indoor background noise levels in octave band form called Preferred Noise Criteria (PNC) curves. (Source. L. L. Beranek, W. E. Blazier, and J. J. Figwer, "Preferred Noise Criteria Curves and Their Applications to Rooms" J. Ac. Soc. Am., Vol. 50, No. 5, 1971.)

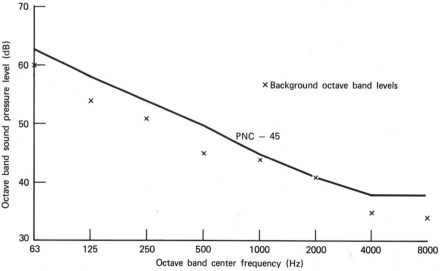

FIGURE 7.10 Example of measured background octave band levels that satisfy a PNC-45 curve.

TABLE 7.1
Design Objectives for Indoor A-Weighted Sound Levels in Rooms with Various Uses

Type or Use of Space	Approximate A-Weighted Sound Level (dBA)
Concert halls, opera houses, recital halls	21 to 30
Large auditoriums, large drama theaters, churches (for excellent listening conditions)	Not above 30
Broadcast, television, and recording studios	Not above 34
Small auditoriums, small theaters, small churches, music rehearsal rooms, large meeting and conference rooms (for good listening)	Not above 42
Bedrooms, sleeping quarters, hospitals, residences, apartments, hotels, motels (for sleeping, resting, relaxing)	34 to 47
Private or semiprivate offices, small conference rooms, classrooms, libraries, etc. (for good listening conditions)	38 to 47
Living rooms and similar spaces in dwellings (for conversing or listening to radio and television)	38 to 47
Large offices, reception areas, retail shops and stores, cafeterias, restaurants, etc. (moderately good listening)	42 to 52
Lobbies, laboratory work spaces, drafting and engineering rooms, general secretarial areas (for fair listening conditions)	47 to 56
Light maintenance shops, office and computer equipment rooms, kitchens, laundries (moderately fair listening conditions)	52 to 61
Shops, garages, power-plant control rooms, etc. (for just-acceptable speech and telephone communication)	56 to 66

Source. L. L. Beranek, W. E. Blazier, and J. J. Figwer, "Preferred Noise Criteria (PNC) Curves and their Application to Rooms," *J. Acoust. Soc. Am.* 50, 1223–1228 (1971)."

7.3 **Sleep Interference**

Physiological measurements of people tested under laboratory conditions show that there are four stages of sleep, ranging from a drowsiness stage to a deep sleep stage. Electroencephalograms (EEG) provide recordings of brain waves that classify the stages of sleep as:

Stage 1—drowsiness (alpha waves).
Stage 2—rapid eye movement (beta waves).
Stages 3 and 4—deep sleep (delta waves).

From experimentation it has been learned that noise can alter the stage of sleep so that we may awake or at least shift our sleep from one stage to another. The arousal from sleep because of noise depends on several factors associated with the noise level and the individual. Such factors include the intensity of the noise, the degree of fluctuation of the noise, the depth of sleep, the individual's motivation to awake, the accumulated sleep, the previous sleep deprivation, and other individual differences (age, sex, drugs, etc.). For example, fluctuating noise is more likely to arouse us from sleep than steady-state noise. Also, middle-aged women tend to be lighter sleepers than middle-aged men.

The heating and air conditioning industry reports[3] that nighttime bedroom sound levels of 33 to 38 dBA produce occasional complaints, while levels above 48 dBA result in numerous complaints. Others have found that the probability of being awakened by a peak sound level of 40 dBA is 5 percent, increasing to 30 percent at 70 dBA. In the range of 100 to 120 dBA, nearly everyone awakens. Table 7.1 indicates that rooms used for sleeping quarters should be designed for an approximate range of 34 to 47 dBA. What level is actually chosen for a given situation will be governed by many factors, not the least of which will be cost considerations.

It should be emphasized that sleep interference studies from noise is based on limited laboratory experiments. Consequently, the long-term effects of sleep loss is unknown as a health hazard. However, frequent sleep interference may be a health hazard, since we are deprived of the restorative process for our organs to renew their supply of energy and nutritive elements provided by a good night's sleep. The loss of sleep from noise affects our personal well-being and, perhaps, our job performance. Should we be subjected to unrelenting noise conditions, it most certainly will adversely affect our mental and physical health.

7.4 Annoyance

Hardly a day passes without being subjected to some intruding noise. Why we are annoyed and to what degree depend on many factors, some of which are:

- The characteristics of the noise—intensity, frequency spectra, time duration.
- Interruptions from the noise—trying to concentrate, watching TV, and so forth.
- Our personal sensitivity to noise—2 to 10 percent of the population are highly susceptible to noise not of their own making, while approximately 20 percent are unaffected by noise.
- Our attitude toward the noise source—is it our dog that's barking or our neighbor's dog?
- Whether we believe someone is trying to abate the noise—has a local noise ordinance been recently adopted?

There have been a number of rating methods developed over the years in an attempt to correlate man's level of annoyance from noise with certain measureable quantities. Some of these quantities used in developing a rating method include:

- The sound intensity level and duration of the noise.
- The number of occurrences of a major noise source during some predetermined time period, such as the daytime, nighttime, and so on.
- The existing background noise level in the community.
- The degree of the noise level fluctuations.
- The time of day when the noise occurs.
- Special characteristics of the noise such as the presence of pure tones.

The details to develop rating methods will be examined later. For now, let us consider Figure 7.11, which shows the expected community reaction as a function of three such rating methods: the community noise equivalent level (CNEL), the noise exposure forecast (NEF), and the composite noise

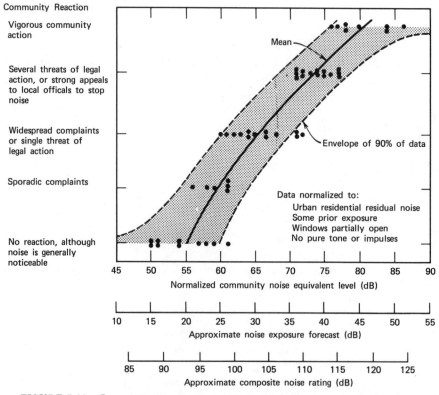

FIGURE 7.11 *Community response to environmental noise as measured in terms of standard rating methods. (Source. "Community Noise," NTID 300.3, EPA, December 1971.)*

rating (CNR). Each of these three methods are shown to be approximately related along the abscissa axis in Figure 7.11. Based on a number of social surveys, the expected community reaction for a given noise level is indicated on the ordinate axis, ranging from essentially no reaction up to vigorous community action. For example, if the noise level in a residential community is equivalent to an NEF level equal to 30, the mean curve indicates that widespread complaints or a single threat of legal action may be expected by those responsible for the noise. This type of information is particularly useful for land use planning, such as locating a new commercial airport.

7.5 Task Interference

The effects of noise on the human performance of tasks is a complicated subject that is under continued study. In those situations requiring an audible sound to perform a job, noise of any intensity can interfere with the completion of the task. However, when mental or motor tasks do not involve audible sounds, the noise effects on their performance have been difficult to assess.[4,5] This is because human behavior is complicated, and it is difficult to assess how different kinds of noise affect different kinds of people doing different kinds of tasks.

The following summarizes certain general conclusions that can be made on the subject.[4]

1. Steady noises without special meaning do not seem to interfer with human performance unless the A-weighted noise level exceeds about 90 decibels.
2. Irregular bursts of noise are more disruptive than steady noises. Even when the A-weighted sound levels of irregular bursts are below 90 decibels, they may sometimes interfere with performance of a task.
3. High-frequency components of noise, above about 1000-2000 Hz, may produce more interference with performance than low-frequency components of noise.
4. Noise does not seem to influence the overall rate of work, but high levels of noise may increase the variability of the rate of work. There may be "noise pauses" followed by compensating increases in work rate.
5. Noise is more likely to reduce the accuracy of work than to reduce the total quantity of work.
6. Complex tasks are more likely to be adversely influenced by noise than are simple tasks.

7.6 Other Effects

The lack of acoustical privacy has been frequently experienced by people living in new multifamily dwellings built with lightweight construction materials. These people have been upset in finding themselves living in a glass house, acoustic-wise. Local government building codes should be updated to improve this unfortunate situation. Incorporating minimum STC levels between various types of rooms, as shown earlier in Table 5.3, appears to be a desirable step in the right direction. For example, the U.S. Department of Housing and Urban Development (HUD) in its 1971 Circular 1390.2 prescribes this approach for floors and dividing walls between family units in multifamily structures. The HUD Circular regards an STC rating below 45 as unacceptable in order to receive approval for HUD funding.

It is believed that people suffer psychological stress from excess exposure to high noise levels over extended periods of time. While this may be true in some cases, there is no conclusive evidence that exposure to noise can result in mental illness. Likewise, speculation has persisted that noise may contribute to circulatory problems and heart disease. Although there is no scientific data to support these claims conclusively,[3] it is interesting to observe the results of one study, shown in Figure 7.12. Here we see the difference between the percent of occurrence of certain physiological problems between industrial workers exposed to two different levels of noise. Clearly, those receiving the greater noise exposure have the higher occurrence of physiological problems.

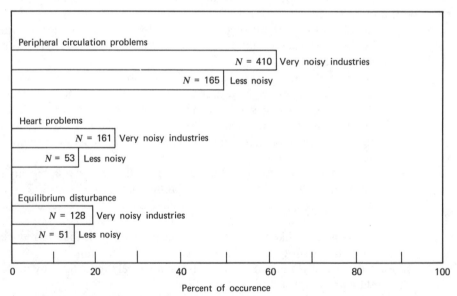

FIGURE 7.12   Differences between the percentages of physiological problems of those who work in two different levels of noise. These data are for 1005 German industrial workers. (Source. K. D. Kryter, G. Jansen, D. Parker, H. O. Parrack, G. Thiessen, and H. L. Williams, "Non-Auditory Effects of Noise," Report of WG-63, NAS-NRC CHABA, Washington, D.C.)

7.7 Summary

The important ideas:

1. Chronic exposure to sounds may lead to permanent hearing threshold shifts, depending on the source intensity, frequency content, and time duration.
2. Outdoor speech interference is related to voice level, distance between persons, and background noise level in dBA.
3. Sleep interference from noise has been studied primarily in laboratory situations using EEG measurements of brain waves.
4. Annoyance from noise is affected by people's attitudes and personal sensitivity to the noise source.
5. Rating methods have been developed to correlate community response to measureable quantities associated with the noise.
6. Continued research is being performed to relate psychological and physiological effects from noise on man.

7.8 Assignments

7.1 Have an audiogram taken on your hearing at your local Speech and Hearing Clinic.

7.2 Explain what is meant by noise-induced cochlea injury.

7.3 What is presbycusis?

7.4 What is acoustic trauma?

7.5 Explain preferred speech interference level.

7.6 What is the PSIL for the octave band data shown in Figure 7.10?

7.7 If two people are 1 m apart outdoors, what is the recommended maximum background noise in A-weighted sound pressure level for relaxed conversation (sentence intelligibility = 99 percent)?

7.8 Repeat problem 7.7 if the individuals are speaking at normal voice.

7.9 What are the stages of sleep and how are they determined?

7.10 Discuss the factors that explain our disposition to sleep interference from noise.

7.11 What is the range in dBA levels recommended by the heating and air conditioning industry for nighttime bedroom noise that produce occasional complaints? How do these compare with the recommendations in Table 7.1?

7.12 List some of the factors that affect our level of annoyance from noise.

7.13 What are some of the quantities taken into consideration in developing noise rating schemes?

7.14 Interview at least 10 acquaintances to ascertain their attitudes on the effects of noise on their hearing, sleep, and speech communication.

7.15 Conduct a survey of at least 10 people to determine what kinds of noise annoy them and to what degree.

7.16 What are the general conclusions that can be made concerning the effects of noise on human task performance?

References

[1] G. Chedd, *Sound*, Doubleday, 1970.

[2] L. L. Beranek, *Noise and Vibration Control*, Chapter 17, McGraw-Hill, 1971.

[3] "Public Health and Welfare Criteria for Noise," U.S. Environmental Protection Agency, July 27 1973.

[4] "Effects of Noise on People," U.S. Environmental Protection Agency, NTID 300.7, p. 118–119, December 31 1971.

[5] K. Kryter, *The Effects of Noise on Man*, Academic Press, 1970.

8
SPECIAL NOISE ENVIRONMENTS

Situations occur where people are exposed to sounds that lie outside the audible range or to audible sounds that are particularly short in time duration. The former include infrasounds and ultrasounds, while the latter include impulse sounds, such as the sonic boom. We shall explore these special types of sounds along with a brief examination of the effects of noise on animals. It will be apparent that much of the subject matter in this chapter is still under investigation, so that any recommended levels prescribed are tentative until more information is known about the health effects of these special noise environments.

8.1 Infrasound

The fundamental frequencies of the pipe organ range from 16 to 8000 Hz, this being the widest frequency range of any musical instrument. Sounds whose frequencies are less than 16 Hz are called infrasounds. Although these sounds are not in the audible frequency range, their presence can sometimes be felt. Some natural sources that generate infrasounds include the surf pounding on the beach, earthquakes, thunder, and wind turbulence. Some man-made sources include heating and air conditioning systems, jet aircraft, and space craft during blast-off.

Researchers have found[1] that when people are exposed to infrasounds under laboratory conditions, they may experience difficulties in performing mental work as well as a general sense of discomfort. As the intensity increases, dizziness, nervous fatigue, nausea, and loss of balance have been experienced by these same individuals. At still higher intensities, a person's internal organs will vibrate, causing pain and possibly death. In the case of naturally produced infrasounds, some hypothesize that people and animals are visibly upset before some natural disaster, like an earthquake, due to the infrasounds that precede the arrival of the catastrophy. Others have attempted to correlate school absenteeism and automobile accidents with infrasounds produced by storms many miles away. A program has been underway in France[2] to develop weapons that utilize infrasound. Here, large massive pipes generate infrasonic sounds, much like a police whistle generates sounds. By focusing the infrasound, the released energy is so great that it is capable of demolishing buildings and people that may lie along its path.

As far as our hearing mechanism is concerned, a sample of some current research results shown in Table 8.1 indicates that little damage is to be expected for infrasonic sounds in real-life situations. Measurements on temporary threshold shifts from infrasound show little, if any, change. Where

TABLE 8.1
Summary of Hearing Response to Infrasound

Investigator	Exposure	Hearing Response	Recovery
Tonndorf	Submarine diesel room 10–20 Hz. No level given	Depression of upper limits of hearing as measured by number of seconds a tuning fork was heard	Recovery in few hours outside of diesel room
Mohr, et al.	Discrete tones: narrow band noise in 10–20 Hz region. 150–154 dB exposures of about 2 minutes	No change in hearing sensitivity reported by subjects; no TTS measured about one hour post exposure	
Jerger, et al.	Successive 3 minute whole body exposures. 7–12 Hz; 119–144 dB	TTS in 3000–6000 Hz range for 11 of 19 subjects (TTS of 10–22 dB)	Recovery within hours
Nixon	Pistonphone coupled to ear via earmuff. 18 Hz at 135 dB. Series of 6, 5 minute exposures rapid in succession	Average TTS of 0–15 dB after 30 minute exposures	Recovery within 30 minutes
Nixon	Pistonphone coupled to ear via earmuff. 14 Hz at 140 dB. Six individual exposures of 5, 10, 15, 20, 25, and 30 minutes	Three experienced subjects: no TTS in one; slight TTS in one; 20–25 dB TTS in one	Recovery within 30 minutes

Source. W. Nixon and D. L. Johnson, "Infrasound and Hearing," International Congress on Noise as a Public Health Problem, Dubrovnik, Yugoslavia, 1973.

threshold shifting occurs, it has been observed that the hearing level returns to its original level rather quickly. The U.S. Environmental Protection Agency (EPA) recommends[3] a threshold level of 120 dB between 1 and 16 Hz as the upper level exposure to infrasound. Caution is urged by EPA in accepting this level, since it is based on research that sometimes included sound energy in the audible frequency range as well as in the infrasonic range.

8.2 Ultrasound

Ultrasounds, whose frequencies are above 20,000 Hz, occur from jet engines, high-speed drills, cleaning devices, and special tools used in the science of ultrasonics. These special tools propagate rays of ultrasound and, by measuring the echo time, an X-ray-like image is produced. This technique has led to many practical uses of ultrasound.

The Germans performed much of the basic research with ultrasound in the 1930s. Many applications of ultrasonic waves followed after World War II. Some of today's applications include ultrasonic cleaning of teeth, detecting flaws in metals, listening to the heart movement of a fetus, and physical therapy. Care should be exercised when using ultrasound for theraputic purposes, since vital organs of the body could be damaged if the intensity is too great.

People have experienced adverse effects from exposure to ultrasound. These effects include excessive fatigue, nausea, headaches, and vomiting when working in the vicinity of ground-tested jet engines that were producing ultrasonic waves. Research in this area is hindered because the high absorption by air of ultrasonic waves requires that the investigation be made close to the source. Likewise, airborne ultrasonics normally are accompanied by sounds in the audible range.

EPA currently recommends[3] ultrasonic levels below 105 dB to avoid a serious health hazard. Once again caution is suggested by EPA with this level, since some of the research data included sound energy in the audible frequency range as well as in the ultrasonic range.

8.3 Impulse Noise

When a hammer strikes a nail or a gun is fired, the sound pressure rises abruptly and then decays over a short time interval. Figure 8.1a shows the pressure-time history of a pure impulse typical of gunfire in free space. Figure 8.1b shows a reverberant or ringing type of impulse noise, which is experienced in industrial situations. Table 8.2 lists typical peak sound pressure levels from impulse noise in real-life examples. Here we see the peak sound pressure levels ranging from 110 dB to as high as 190 dB. It is

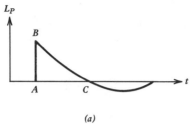
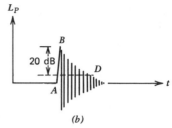

FIGURE 8.1   *Sound pressure level variations as a function of time caused by (a) non-reverberant impulse, (b) reverberant impulse noise.*

interesting to observe that the examples in Table 8.2 refer not only to military and occupational environments, but also to recreational uses of hand guns, toy caps, and firecrackers.

To assess potential hearing damage from impulse noise, we should consider the peak pressure magnitude, the time duration, and the number of impulses per unit time, and we should account for the duration of ringing.[4] If the number of impulses exceeds 10 per second, simply treat the noise as continuous instead of impulsive.

Figure 8.2 shows tentative recommended[3] peak sound pressure levels as a function of the impulse time duration. The curves labeled AC-duration and AD-duration correspond to the impulse signatures shown in Figure 8.1a and 8.1b, respectively. Here we observe a reduction in the peak pressure level with an increase in time duration for either type of impulse. In the case of a pure impulse, a maximum peak pressure of 140 dB is recommended for a time exposure greater than 1.5 ms, while in the case of reverberant impulse

TABLE 8.2
Some Typical Values of Peak Sound Pressure Levels for Impulse Noise

Sound Pressure Level (dB)	Example
190+	Within blast zone of exploding bomb
160–180	Within crew area of heavy artillery piece or naval gun when shooting
140–170	At shooter's ear when firing hand gun
125–160	At child's ear when detonating toy cap or firecracker
120–140	Metal to metal impacts in many industrial processes (e.g., drop-forging, metal-beating)
110–130	On construction site during pile-driving

Source. "Information on Levels of Environmental Noise Requisite to Protect Public Health and Welfare with an Adequate Margin of Safety," EPA, 1974.

120   SPECIAL NOISE ENVIRONMENTS

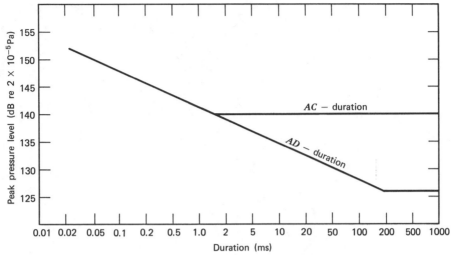

FIGURE 8.2   Recommended peak sound pressure level as a function of time duration for impulse noise. (*Source. "Information on Levels of Environmental Noise Requisite to Protect Public Health and Welfare with an Adequate Margin of Safety," EPA, March 1974.*)

noise, the maximum peak pressure levels off at 126 dB for an exposure time greater than 200 ms.

The criteria shown in Figure 8.2 have been selected by EPA to protect 90 percent of the people exposed to impulse noise from a hearing loss of 5 dB at 4000 Hz after 10 years of repeated exposure. However, the peak pressure level obtained from Figure 8.2 must be modified according to the following rules to obtain the recommended level.

- Use Figure 8.3 to correct for the number of impulses experienced per day. From this figure we observe that 100 impulses carries no correction, while we increase or decrease the peak pressure level for less than or greater than 100 impulses per day, respectively.
- If the average interval between impulses is from 1 to 10 s, reduce the peak level by 5 dB. (This occurs in industrial situations such as metal-beating and pile driving.)
- If the sound reaches the ear at grazing incidence, increase the peak level by 5 dB. (If in a reverberent sound field, do not make this correction.)

Example 8.1
Find the recommended peak pressure level for the pure impulse in Figure 8.1*a* if the AC-duration equals (a) 50 ms, (b) 0.5 ms, and (c) 0.05 ms. Assume 1000 impulses per day in each case and normal incidence of sound reaching the ear.

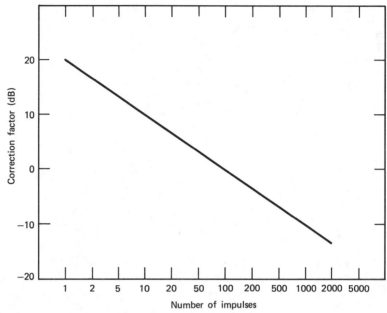

FIGURE 8.3   Correction factor to be added to the recommended peak sound pressure level as a function of the number of impulses per day. (Source. "Information on Levels of Environmental Noise Requisite to Protect Public Health and Welfare with an Adequate Margin of Safety," EPA, March 1974.)

From Figure 8.3 we observe that for 1000 impulses per day the correction factor is −10 dB. There is no further correction for this sound for grazing, since it reaches the ear at normal incidence. Referring to Figure 8.2 and applying the −10 dB correction, the following results are obtained.

(a) 140 dB − 10 dB = 130 dB   Answer
(b) 143 dB − 10 dB = 133 dB   Answer
(c) 150 dB − 10 dB = 140 dB   Answer

8.4 Sonic Boom

When an aircraft's speed exceeds the speed of sound, sound waves cannot move ahead of the aircraft. Cone-shaped shock waves are formed that move outward much like water waves from a ship's bow. Figure 8.4 shows the two incident shock waves that normally reach the earth's surface. In this case we may hear two sharp bangs associated with the two shock wave fronts separated by a short time interval. Measurements made with the microphone flush to the ground show an N-pressure wave characterization of the total sonic boom, as shown in Figure 8.5a. The pressure change associated with

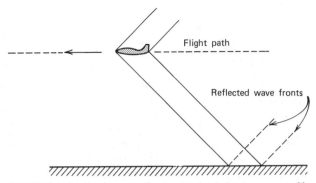

FIGURE 8.4 *Bow wave and tail wave shock fronts generated by a supersonic jet aircraft.*

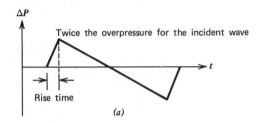

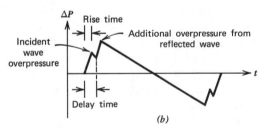

FIGURE 8.5 *Variation of overpressure caused by (a) incident shock wave plus reflected shock wave with microphone flush to the ground, (b) incident shock wave plus reflected shock wave with the microphone above ground.*

the incident wave is added to the pressure change due to the reflected wave, so that the measured peak overpressure is approximately twice that of the incident wave. If the microphone is above ground, the reflected wave introduces a delay time, as indicated in Figure 8.5b.

As the aircraft travels at supersonic speed, a "boom carpet" is swept across the earth's surface by the shock wave fronts, as shown in Figure 8.6. It should be understood that this is a continuing process as long as the

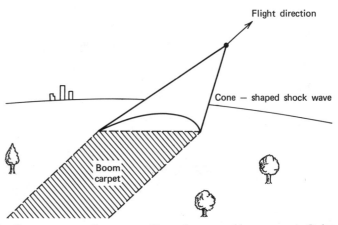

FIGURE 8.6 *Boom carpet trail across earth's surface caused by supersonic flight.*

aircraft speed exceeds the speed of sound. People living within the boom carpet, which may be 30 to 130 km wide for the first-generation SST[5], experience the sonic boom, while those living closely outside the boom carpet will hear a rumbling sound.

The startling effect of sonic booms on people is perhaps one of the major criticisms leveled at the SST. The actual loudness of the boom is affected by the initial rise time and delay time, which may range within 0.1 to 16 ms. The overall duration of the sonic boom lasts between 100 to 500 ms. Most of the energy associated with the boom is contained in the infrasonic range. Consequently, structures possessing a corresponding natural frequency of oscillation may be set into resonance and produce severe structural damage. Other factors that may produce magnified overpressures from sonic booms include aircraft maneuvering at low altitude, variations in the sonic boom signature, and the aircraft accelerating from subsonic to supersonic speed.

Government studies[6] report that damage to residential windows, plaster walls, and artifacts occurred during supersonic flight tests made during the 1960s. Of the 9489 claims filed by individuals for sonic boom damage, 2556 were acceptable to government inspectors. The average paid-out damage per million boom-person-exposure was $222, where a boom-person-exposure represents the experience of one sonic boom by one person. In addition to the startling effect on people and structural damage to buildings, concern also exists that sonic booms might trigger avalanches, landslides, and damage archeological findings.

Based on field measurements of people's response to varying magnitudes of sonic boom overpressures, EPA[3] states that "little or no public annoyance is expected to result from one sonic boom during the daytime below the level of 35.91 Pa as measured on the ground." This pressure level is based on a day-night average level of 55 dB, which is explained in Chapter 9. For more than one boom per day EPA recommends that the peak level of each boom be no greater than:

$$\text{peak level} = \frac{35.91}{\sqrt{N}}, \quad \text{Pa} \tag{8.1}$$

in which N equals the number of booms. This relationship can be used to express the maximum overpressure in dB as follows.

$$L_p = 10 \log \frac{p^2}{p_o{}^2} = 10 \log \frac{(35.91)^2}{Np_o{}^2} = 125 - 10 \log N \tag{8.2}$$

We observe that as the number of daily sonic booms doubles, the maximum recommended overpressure decreases by 3 dB.

8.5 Effects of Noise on Animals

Guinea pigs, rats, chinchillas, dogs, and cats are favored animals for noise effect studies. These animals are usually subjected to intense sound levels over relatively short periods of time instead of low levels over long time periods. From these tests, researchers have been able to observe damage done to the animal's hearing mechanism, blood chemistry, and stress response.

Most farm animals show good adjustments to noise, particularly the larger animals such as horses, cattle, and swine. However, poultry are not as adaptable to sounds, particularly to unexpected loud sounds. In fact, one of the earliest recorded official complaints[7] related to aircraft noise occurred in 1928 when a farmer wrote to the Postmaster General complaining that low-flying aircraft were disrupting egg production.

There are practically no data available on controlled tests of wildlife under realistic, chronic exposures to noise.[6] It would be useful in understanding the noise effects on wildlife, particularly with regard to animal panic behavior, affects on exploratory behavior, prey-predator relationships, and mating signals.

8.6 Summary

A. The important ideas:
1. Both infrasound and ultrasound can be health hazards if the pressure levels are high enough and the time exposures long enough.
2. There is limited information on human effects from impulse noise, although tentative guidelines on recommended exposures do exist.

3. When an aircraft flies at supersonic speed, it creates two cone-shaped shock wave fronts that sweep across the terrain, forming a "boom carpet."
4. While much has been learned on auditory damage to animals tested in laboratory experiments, little is known on noise effects on farm animals and even less is known on wildlife.

B. The important equation:

$$L_p = 125 - 10 \log N \tag{8.2}$$

8.7 Assignments

8.1 List some natural sources and man-made sources of infrasound.

8.2 Describe the effects experienced by people exposed to high levels of infrasound.

8.3 What are the EPA recommended sound pressure level thresholds for infrasound and for ultrasound, respectively, to avoid health hazards?

8.4 Research one practical application of ultrasonics and write a short paper on your findings.

8.5 Describe the effects experienced by people subject to ultrasound near ground tested jet engines.

8.6 What is the allowable peak pressure exposure for the impulse sound shown in Figure 8.7 if it is repeated 50 times daily?

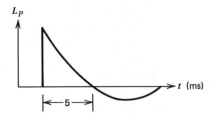

FIGURE 8.7   Problem 8.6.

8.7 Repeat problem 8.6, assuming that the impulse is repeated 500 times daily and at a grazing incidence on the ear.

8.8 How many times must an impulse occur per second before the sound is treated as continuous sound?

8.9 What average time interval between impulses produces a 5-dB reduction in the peak sound pressure level?

8.10 Is the pressure-time history in Figure 8.8 that occurs 100 times daily within the EPA recommendation on impulse noise?

8.11 Repeat problem 8.10, assuming that the impulse noise occurs once daily at a grazing incidence on the ear.

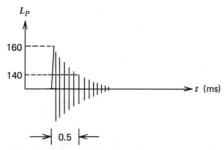

FIGURE 8.8   Problem 8.10.

8.12 Distinguish between the overpressure signatures from sonic booms for measurements made flush to the ground and above ground.

8.13 What is meant by the boom carpet from supersonic overflights?

8.14 List some of the factors that contribute to magnifying a sonic boom overpressure.

8.15 What is the recommended peak pressure from supersonic flights over a community if six daily flights are anticipated? Express your result in decibels.

8.16 Read one paper written on laboratory experimentation with animals subjected to noise and summarize your findings.

References

[1] "Public Health and Welfare Criteria for Noise," U.S. Environmental Protection Agency, Section 10, July 27 1973.

[2] G. Chedd, *Sound*, Chapter 6, Doubleday, 1970.

[3] "Information on Levels of Environmental Noise Requisite to Protect Public Health and Welfare with an Adequate Margin of Safety," U.S. Environmental Protection Agency, March 1974.

[4] L. L. Beranek, *Noise and Vibration Control*, Chapter 17, McGraw-Hill, 1971.

[5] J. T. Broch, *Acoustic Noise Measurements*, Chapter 5, Bruel & Kjaer, 1971.

[6] "Report to the President and Congress on Noise," U.S. Environmental Protection Agency, Chapter 1, February 1972.

[7] FAA Historic Fact Book, 1966.

9
OUTDOOR COMMUNITY NOISE

The type of community generally reflects its environmental noise climate. For example, rural areas tend to be quieter than urban areas; wealthy communities are quieter than poor communities. Also, in some communities, the noise varies appreciably over a 24-h period, and perhaps may vary from season to season. The characteristics of community noise not only include the intensity and frequency spectrum of the noise, but also its temporal pattern. We shall consider some of the rating methods that have been developed to establish quantitatively the outdoor community noise climate. These rating methods allow a community to categorize its noise climate, to develop evidence in assessing noise control efforts, and to provide long-term environmental noise level trends.

9.1 Examples of Community Noise

Figure 9.1 is a sample of outdoor noise in a suburban neighborhood with the microphone located 20 ft from the street curb. The A-weighted network was selected to account for the frequency characteristics of the measured noise, which is normally done in outdoor measurements. It is apparent from the figure that the sound pressure level varies appreciably over the 8-min period shown. We observe that approximately 80 s elapse during the aircraft overflight, while 5 to 20 s elapse for the passing cars. Consequently, we might expect the aircraft noise to be judged noisier, not only due to higher intensity levels but also to the longer time exposure. Also, the degree of annoyance experienced by community residents will be affected by the number of times the exposure occurs throughout a 24-h period, and particularly if any occur at night.

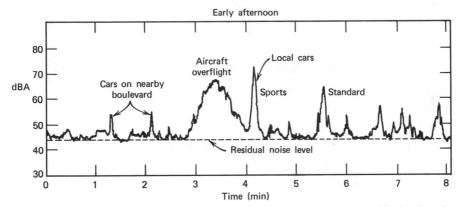

FIGURE 9.1 Outdoor community noise variation in a suburban neighborhood in the early afternoon. (Source. "Community Noise," NTID 300.3 EPA, December 1971.)

While the details in Figure 9.1 are useful to portray community noise, we soon realize that it becomes impractical to show the noise continuously over a 24-h period. We need some way to quantify the noise environment that fluctuates so much. Before examining these techniques, however, it is helpful to be familiar with the following definitions.

Ambient noise. This is the total noise associated with a given environment and usually comprises sounds from many sources both near and far. This is the noise that we are examining in this chapter.

Background noise. This is a noise without a particular noise source in operation.

Steady-state noise. This noise fluctuates less than 6 dB in range with the sound level meter on the slow setting.[1] The average level can be read from the meter after a 10-s observation.

9.2 Some Statistical Indicators

Consider a portion of a sample of the recorded noise level in Figure 9.2. Let us count the number of times the sound levels occur in selected decibel-increments, say 5 dB, at 1-s intervals. This is shown in the figure only for the increment between 65 and 70 dBA for clarity, which shows a count of six. Having such a count for the entire recording time between 65 and 70 dBA as well as for the remaining 5-dB increments, we can plot the data in the form of a histogram. For each 5-dB increment we may plot the actual number of counts or, more preferably, the percent of the time each 5-dB increment occurred. Suppose, for example, we obtain the histogram in Figure 9.3. This may be developed from selected time sampling increments such as 1 s, or

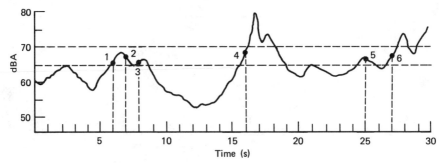

FIGURE 9.2   Sampling of community noise between 65 and 70 dBA in 1-s increments.

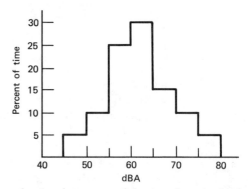

FIGURE 9.3   Example of a histogram showing the percent of the time the noise level is within 5-dBA intervals.

perhaps it may be developed from a shorter or longer time sampling increment. In any event, the percent of the time a noise interval exists over the entire sample period is plotted in the histogram by a horizontal line whose width is equal to the corresponding decibel increment.

Having the histogram, we calculate the percent of time a noise level is exceeded during the sample period. The following are typical statistical quantities.

L_{10}—the sound pressure level exceeded 10 percent of the time.
L_{50}—the sound pressure level exceeded 50 percent of the time.
L_{90}—the sound pressure level exceeded 90 percent of the time.

The L_{50} is normally equal to the mean noise level throughout the measured period, while the L_{90} is sometimes called the residual noise level. In some cases, such as highway noise, an L_{10} is an indication of the level of annoyance from the noise.

Figure 9.4 shows the results of 24-h outdoor noise levels in statistical form for 18 locations around the country. The results include the levels

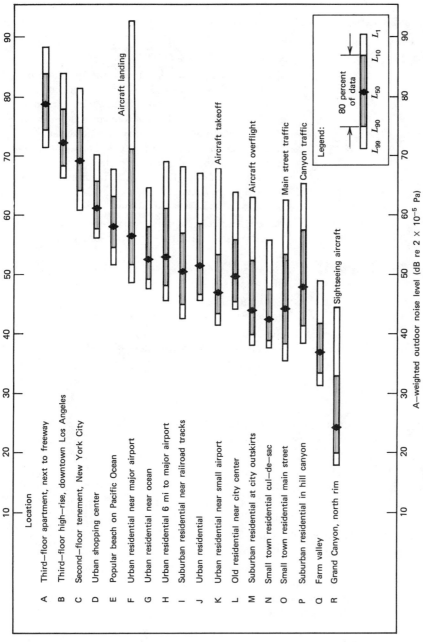

FIGURE 9.4 Twenty-four hour outdoor noise levels found in 18 locations ranging between the wilderness and the downtown city, with significant intruding sources noted. Data are arithmetic averages of the 24 hourly values in the entire day of the levels that are exceeded 99, 90, 50, 10, and 1 percent of the time. (Source. "Community Noise," NTID 300.3, EPA, December 1971.)

TABLE 9.1
Design Noise Level/Land Use Relationships

Land Use Category	Design Noise Level—L_{10}	Description of Land Use Category
A	60 dBA (exterior)	Tracts of lands in which serenity and quiet are of extraordinary significance and serve an important public need, and where the preservation of those qualities is essential if the area is to continue to serve its intended purpose. Such areas could include amphitheaters, particular parks or portions of parks, or open spaces which are dedicated or recognized by appropriate local officials for activities requiring special qualities of serenity and quiet.
B	70 dBA (exterior)	Residences, motels, hotels, public meeting rooms, schools, churches, libraries, hospitals, picnic areas, recreation areas, playgrounds, active sports areas, and parks.
C	75 dBA (exterior)	Developed lands, properties or activities not included in categories A and B above.
D	—	For requirements on undeveloped lands see paragraphs 5.a.(5) and (6) of PPM 90-2.
E	55 dBA (interior)	Residences, motels, hotels, public meeting rooms, schools, churches, libraries, hospitals and auditoriums.

Source. FHWA Policy and Procedure Memorandum 90-2, April 1972.

exceeded 99 percent of the time, L_{99}, up to the level exceeded 1 percent of the time, L_1. We observe from the figure that not only is there a wide variation in the noise levels for the different locations, but also a wide decibel range for some of the sites. For example, site F, the urban residence near a major airport, has an L_{99} as low as 48 dBA and an L_1 as high as 92 dBA. This wide range in the statistical noise levels is an undesirable situation that may lead many inhabitants to react unfavorably to the airport operations.

In April 1972 noise level standards were issued by the Federal Highway Administration as Policy and Procedure Memorandum (PPM) 90-2, which adopted the L_{10} as the principal statistical indicator for evaluating the noise impact from highway traffic. Table 9.1 summarizes recommended L_{10} levels that should not be exceeded during the noisiest hour of the day in the design year for a major highway. For example, when a planned highway reaches its maximum traffic capacity, the L_{10} should not exceed 70 dBA in residential areas during the busiest hour of the day.

The Federal Housing and Urban Development Agency (HUD) has issued maximum noise levels in neighborhoods where federal loans will be provided. Table 9.2 summarizes the HUD Circular 1390.2 for external noise

TABLE 9.2
External Noise Exposure Standards for New Construction Sites

General External Exposures	Airport Environs	
dBA	CNR Zone	NEF Zone
Unacceptable		
Exceeds 80 dBA 60 min per 24 h	3	C
Exceeds 75 dBA 8 h per 24 h		
[Exceptions are strongly discouraged and require a 102(2)C environmental statement and the Secretary's approval]		
Discretionary—Normally Unacceptable		
Exceeds 65 dBA 8 h per 24 h	2	B
Loud repetitive sounds on site		
[Approvals require noise attenuation measures, the Regional Administrator's concurrence and a 102(2)C environmental statement]		
Discretionary—Normally Acceptable		
Does not exceed 65 dBA more than 8 h per 24 h		
Acceptable		
Does not exceed 45 dBA more than 30 min per 24 h	1	A

Source. U.S. Dept. of Housing & Urban Development, Policy Circular 1390.2, 1971.

standards for new construction sites. Here we observe dBA levels that are not to exceed 60 min per 24 h, 8 h per 24 h, and 30 min per 24 h. For example, a site is unacceptable if 75 dBA is exceeded 8 h per 24 h which, in effect, is an L_{33} over the 24-h period.

Example 9.1
Calculate the L_{10}, L_{50}, and L_{90} for the histogram in Figure 9.3.
   First calculate the area under the histogram.

$$\text{Area} = 5(5 + 10 + 25 + 30 + 15 + 10 + 5) = 500$$

L_{90} calculation: Equate 10 percent of the area under the histogram starting from the left to 10 percent of the total area. Referring to Figure 9.5a,

$$5(5) + 10x = 0.1(500)$$
$$x = 2.5$$

Therefore,

$$L_{90} = 50 + 2.5 = 52.5 \text{ dBA} \qquad \text{Answer}$$

L_{50} calculation: Equate 50 percent of the area under the histogram starting

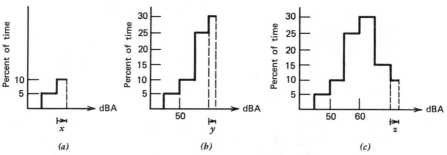

FIGURE 9.5   Portions of a histogram to find (a) L_{90}, (b) L_{50}, and (c) L_{10}.

from the left to 50 percent of the total area. Referring to Figure 9.5b,

$$5(5 + 10 + 25) + 30y = 0.5(500)$$
$$y = 1.67$$

Therefore,

$$L_{50} = 60 + 1.7 = 61.7 \text{ dBA} \qquad \text{Answer}$$

L_{10} calculation: Equate 90 percent of the area under the histogram starting from the left to 90 percent of the total area. Referring to Figure 9.5c,

$$5(5 + 10 + 25 + 30 + 15) + 10z = 0.9(500)$$
$$z = 2.5$$

Therefore,

$$L_{10} = 70 + 2.5 = 72.5 \text{ dBA} \qquad \text{Answer}$$

9.3 Energy Equivalent Sound Level

The energy equivalent sound level, L_{eq}, equals the constant sound level whose acoustic energy is equivalent to the acoustic energy of a fluctuating sound over some time interval. For example, suppose the sound pressure level varies during a 1-h period, as shown in Figure 9.6; that is, it equals 80 dBA during the first half hour and 70 dBA during the second half hour. The equivalent energy during this period is *not* 75 dBA but, instead, 77.4 dBA. To arrive at this conclusion, we use the following expression.

$$L_{eq} = 10 \log \left(\sum_{i=1}^{n} f_i \, 10^{L_i/10} \right) \qquad (9.1)$$

in which f_i is the fraction of the time the constant level L_i is present. We note that $10^{L_i/10}$ is proportional to sound energy since, from the definition of the

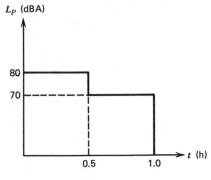

L_P (dBA)

80

70

0.5　　　　1.0　　t (h)

FIGURE 9.6　*Assumed sound pressure level variation for a 1-h duration.*

sound pressure level,

$$L_p = 10 \log \frac{p^2}{p_o{}^2}$$

or

$$10^{L_p/10} = \frac{p^2}{p_o{}^2}$$

But p^2 is directly proportional to the sound energy, as shown earlier by Equation 2.9.

Applying Equation 9.1 to the example in Figure 9.6, we observe that each constant sound pressure level lasts for 1/2 of the time. Thus,

$$f_1 = 0.5 \qquad L_1 = 80 \text{ dBA}$$
$$f_2 = 0.5 \qquad L_2 = 70 \text{ dBA}$$

Substituting into Equation 9.1,

$$\begin{aligned}
L_{eq} &= 10 \log (f_1\, 10^{L_1/10} + f_2\, 10^{L_2/10}) \\
&= 10 \log [(0.5)10^8 + (0.5)10^7] \\
&= 10 \log [(5.5)10^7] = 10 \log 5.5 + 10 \log 10^7 \\
&= 7.4 + 70 = 77.4 \text{ dBA}
\end{aligned}$$

In these calculations we are, in effect, adding numbers that are proportional to the corresponding sound energies. The energy associated with the 80 dBA level is 10 times greater than the energy associated with the 70 dBA level. Hence, the L_{eq} equals 77.4 dBA instead of the arithmetic average over the 1-h period of 75 dBA.

It is not necessary for the sound pressure levels to be continuously constant as in the example in Figure 9.6. The same result is obtained if the 80 dBA level occurred during the first 10 min, followed by 25 min of 70 dBA, 15 min of 80 dBA, 5 min of 70 dBA, and 5 min of 80 dBA. Half of the time is still at 80 dBA and the other half is at 70 dBA, regardless of the order. Consequently, the L_{eq} remains 77.4 dBA.

Example 9.2
Given the following constant sound pressure levels and the associated time fractions:

$$L_1 = 80 \text{ dBA} \qquad L_2 = 70 \text{ dBA} \qquad L_3 = 60 \text{ dBA}$$
$$f_1 = 0.2 \qquad\qquad f_2 = 0.4 \qquad\qquad f_3 = 0.4$$

find the energy equivalent sound level.
Using Equation 9.1,

$$\begin{aligned}
L_{eq} &= 10 \log\left[(0.2)10^8 + (0.4)10^7 + (0.4)10^6\right] \\
&= 10 \log(200 \times 10^5 + 40 \times 10^5 + 4 \times 10^5) \\
&= 10 \log(244) + 10 \log 10^5 \\
&= 10(2.387) + 50 = 73.9 \text{ dBA} \qquad \text{Answer}
\end{aligned}$$

9.4 Maximum Levels for a Fraction of the Time

Sometimes a sound source of high intensity and short time duration occurs that effectively establishes the L_{eq} level over a longer time span. Equation 9.1 may be simplified so that we ignore those sounds occurring during the time interval of interest except for the high noise level and its time of occurrence in calculating the L_{eq}. To develop this relationship, consider the noise levels spanning a total time T as shown in Figure 9.7. The high-intensity source of level L_1 lasts for the fraction of the time f_1, while the lower intensity level L_2 lasts for the fraction of the time f_2. Applying Equation 9.1 to this case, the energy equivalent sound level is

$$L_{eq} = 10 \log(f_1\, 10^{L_1/10} + f_2\, 10^{L_2/10})$$

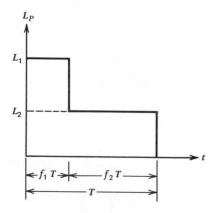

FIGURE 9.7 Assumed sound pressure level variation for a time duration T.

Assuming that

$$f_1 10^{L_1/10} = 10(f_2 10^{L_2/10}) \tag{9.2}$$

then

$$
\begin{aligned}
L_{eq} &= 10 \log[f_1 10^{L_1/10} + (0.1f_1)10^{L_1/10}] \\
&= 10 \log[(1.1f_1)10^{L_1/10}] \\
&= 10 \log 1.1 + 10 \log f_1 + L_1 \\
&= 0.4 + 10 \log f_1 + L_1 \\
&\doteq 10 \log f_1 + L_1
\end{aligned}
\tag{9.3}
$$

Equation 9.3 is an approximation of Equation 9.1 in that the contribution to the L_{eq} from the level L_2 has been deleted subject to the above assumption. If $(f_1 10^{L_1/10}) > 10(f_2 10^{L_2/10})$, the error in Equation 9.3 is even less than 0.4 dB. Whether $(f_1 10^{L_1/10}) \geq 10(f_2 10^{L_2/10})$ will depend on both L_1 and f_1 relative to L_2 and f_2, respectively. For example, if $L_1 = L_2 + 10$, Equation 9.2 yields f_1/f_2 equal to unity. This means that as long as f_1 is equal to or greater than f_2, the error in using Equation 9.3 is equal to or less than 0.4 dB.

Suppose we now substitute $L_1 = L_2 + \Delta$ into Equation 9.2. The resulting relationship between Δ and f_1/f_2 is plotted in Figure 9.8 and is labeled with an error = 0.4 dB. The interpretation of this curve is as follows. For a given Δ, find the corresponding minimum ratio of f_1/f_2 for Equation 9.3 to be

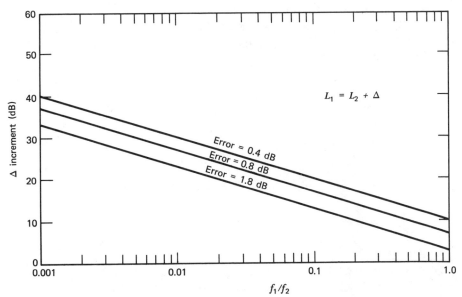

FIGURE 9.8   *Error functions between the increment Δ and the time fraction ratio f_1/f_2 for using Equation 9.3.*

valid subject to an error of 0.4 dB. Conversely, if f_1/f_2 is known, find the corresponding minimum Δ for Equation 9.3 to be valid subject to this error. Of course, similar curves can be generated for other errors one might wish to choose. Figure 9.8 shows two such curves labeled for errors of 0.8 dB and 1.8 dB.

Equation 9.3 is useful in establishing how long a noisy source may operate so as not to exceed a desired L_{eq} over a specified time period. Conversely, knowing how long such a source operates will control the magnitude of the L_{eq}, provided the background level is much quieter.

Example 9.3

If the background level is 70 dBA over a period of time, calculate the L_{eq} using Equation 9.3 if a machine produces 100 dBA for 10 percent of the time.

Let $L_1 = 100$ dBA, $f_1 = 0.1$. Now $f_1/f_2 = 1/9$. From Figure 9.8 we observe that Δ must be at least 19.5 dBA for an error of 0.4 dBA in using Equation 9.3. Since the actual $\Delta = 30$ dBA, we use Equation 9.3 with negligible error being introduced.

$$L_{eq} = \log f_1 + L_1$$
$$= 10 \log 0.1 + 100 = 90 \text{ dBA} \qquad \text{Answer}$$

Example 9.4

How many minutes may a siren operate at 95 dBA over a 24-h period so as not to exceed an L_{eq} of 68 dBA? Assume that a level of 55 dBA exists when the siren is not operating.

In this case, $L_1 = 95$ dBA, $\Delta = 40$ dBA. From Figure 9.8, a minimum value of $f_1/f_2 = 0.001$ is required to use Equation 9.3 for an error of 0.4 dBA. Proceeding with Equation 9.3, we have:

$$L_{eq} = 10 \log f_1 + L_1$$
$$68 = 10 \log f_1 + 95$$
$$\log f_1 = -2.7 = 7.30 - 10$$
$$f_1 = 2.0 \times 10^{-3}$$

Now $f_2 = 1 - f_1 = 0.998$ and $f_1/f_2 = 0.002$. Since this exceeds the minimum allowable value of f_1/f_2, we can complete the solution. The actual time during the 24-h period is calculated.

$$t = f_1(24) = (2.0 \times 10^{-3})(24) = 48 \times 10^{-3} \text{ h} = 2.9 \text{ min} \qquad \text{Answer}$$

9.5 Energy Equivalent Sound Levels from Histograms

Histogram data can be used to calculate an L_{eq}. By way of example, consider the histogram in Figure 9.9. It is recommended by the International Organization for Standardization (ISO) in their publication ISO/R 1996-1971 (E) that

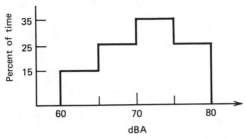

FIGURE 9.9 *Example of a histogram showing the percent of the time the noise level is within 5-dBA intervals.*

the midpoint decibel level be used with Equation 9.1 to represent an assumed constant level during the known fraction of the time. Adopting this recommendation, the data in Figure 9.9 are arranged below in tabular form. Column 1 lists the number of midpoint levels from the histogram; column 2 lists the actual midpoint levels; column 3 includes the time fractions for each level; and the remaining two columns are the computations required for Equation 9.1.

i	L_i	f_i	$10^{L_i/10}$	$f_i\,10^{L_i/10}$
1	62.5	0.15	1.78×10^6	0.267×10^6
2	67.5	0.25	5.62×10^6	$1.41\ \times 10^6$
3	72.5	0.35	$17.8\ \times 10^6$	$6.23\ \times 10^6$
4	77.5	0.25	$56.2\ \times 10^6$	$14.1\ \times 10^6$

$$\sum_{i=1}^{4} f_i\,10^{L_i/10} = 22.007 \times 10^6$$

$$L_{eq} = 10\log(22.0) + 60 = 73.4 \text{ dBA} \qquad \text{Answer}$$

We conclude that during the time interval for which the histogram exists (this may be daytime, nighttime, 24-h period, etc.), a constant sound level of approximately 73.4 dBA contains the same sound energy as actually occurs in the community.

9.6 Day-Night Average Sound Level

Modifications to the L_{eq} have been suggested in the form of penalty levels for sensitive times of the day. For example, the day-night average sound level, L_{dn}, is an L_{eq} A-weighted sound level, during a 24-h period, with a 10 dB penalty for nighttime sound levels. By daytime we mean the time between 7 A.M. to 10 P.M., while nighttime is between 10 P.M. and 7 A.M. For simplicity,

TABLE 9.3
Typical L_{dn} Levels in Outdoor Locations

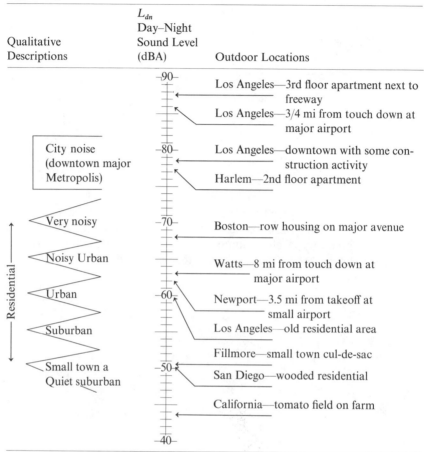

Qualitative Descriptions	L_{dn} Day–Night Sound Level (dBA)	Outdoor Locations
	–90–	Los Angeles—3rd floor apartment next to freeway
		Los Angeles—3/4 mi from touch down at major airport
City noise (downtown major Metropolis)	–80–	Los Angeles—downtown with some construction activity
		Harlem—2nd floor apartment
Very noisy	–70–	Boston—row housing on major avenue
Noisy Urban		Watts—8 mi from touch down at major airport
Urban	–60–	Newport—3.5 mi from takeoff at small airport
Suburban		Los Angeles—old residential area
		Fillmore—small town cul-de-sac
Small town a Quiet suburban	–50–	San Diego—wooded residential
		California—tomato field on farm
	–40–	

Source. "Information on Levels of Environmental Noise Requisite to Protect Public Health and Welfare with an Adequate Margin of Safety," EPA, March 1974.

we refer to the day-night average sound level as the L_{dn}, or simply the "day-night level." Table 9.3 lists typical L_{dn}'s that indicate a wide spread in the levels for different outdoor locations. The number of people in the United States subjected to outdoor L_{dn} levels in residential areas subjected to different kinds of environmental noise is shown in Table 9.4. For example, it is estimated that between 40 and 70 million people live in residential areas that are subjected to urban traffic noise so that the L_{dn} is equal to or greater than 60 dBA.

The U.S. Environment Protection Agency (EPA) has adopted the L_{dn} as the rating method to describe long-term annoyance from environmental

TABLE 9.4

Estimated Number of People (Millions) in Residential Areas Subjected to Noise of Different Kinds at or above Specified L_{dn} Outdoor Levels

Outdoor L_{dn} Level	Urban Traffic Noise	Aircraft Noise	Construction Site Noise	Freeway Noise
70$^+$	4–12	4–7	1–3	1–4
65$^+$	15–33	8–15	3–6	2–5
60$^+$	40–70	16–32	7–15	3–6

Source. Federal Register, Vol. 39, No. 121, page 22297, July 21, 1974.

noise.[2] The recommended L_{dn} is derived from an L_{eq} of 45 dBA within the home, which provides 100 percent intelligibility of speech sounds. Allowing for an average 15-dB reduction with windows partially open, this indoor level becomes 60 dBA outdoors in residential neighborhoods. Finally, this outdoor L_{eq} value is modified to account for other types of annoyance besides speech interference. This is accomplished in two ways, first, by applying a 10-dB nighttime penalty, so that the L_{eq} of 60 dBA becomes an L_{dn} of 60 dBA; and second, a 5-dB margin of safety is introduced. Consequently, EPA recommends an L_{dn} equal to 55 dBA as a desirable outdoor noise level for residential neighborhoods. Table 9.5 summarizes the human

TABLE 9.5

Summary of Human Effects in Terms of Speech Communication, Community Reaction, Complaints, Annoyance and Attitude Towards Area Associated with an Outdoor Day/Night Sound Level of 55 dBA re 2 × 10^{-5} Pa

Type of Effect	Magnitude of Effect
Speech—indoors	100% sentence intelligibility (average) with a 5 dB margin of safety
—outdoors	100% sentence intelligibility (average) at 0.35 m
	99% sentence intelligibility (average) at 1.0 m
	95% sentence intelligibility (average) at 3.5 m
Average community reaction	None evident; 7 dB below level of significant "complaints and threats of legal action" and at least 16 dB below "vigorous action" (attitudes and other nonlevel related factors may affect this result)
Complaints	1% dependent on attitude and other nonlevel related factors
Annoyance	17% dependent on attitude and other nonlevel related factors
Attitudes towards area	Noise essentially the least important of various factors

Source. "Information on Levels of Environmental Noise Requisite to Protect Public Health and Welfare with an Adequate Margin of Safety," EPA, March 1974.

TABLE 9.6
Summary of Noise Levels Identified as Requisite to Protect Public Health and Welfare with an Adequate Margin of Safety

Effect	Level	Area
Hearing Loss	$L_{eq(24)} \leq 70$ dBA	All areas
Outdoor activity interference and annoyance	$L_{dn} \leq 55$ dBA	Outdoors in residential areas and farms and other outdoor areas where people spend widely varying amounts of time and other places in which quiet is a basis for use.
	$L_{eq(24)} \leq 55$ dBA	Outdoor areas where people spend limited amounts of time, such as school yards, playgrounds, etc.
Indoor activity interference and annoyance	$L_{dn} \leq 45$ dBA	Indoor residential areas
	$L_{eq(24)} \leq 45$ dBA	Other indoor areas with human activities such as schools, etc.

Source. "Information on Levels of Environmental Noise Requisite to Protect Public Health and Welfare with an Adequate Margin of Safety," EPA, March 1974.

effects compiled by EPA in terms of speech communication, community reaction, complaints, annoyance, and attitudes towards an area that are attributed to this L_{dn} level.

Table 9.6 is a summary of the levels recommended by EPA for different neighborhoods. Included in this table are 24-h L_{eq}'s, listed as $L_{eq(24)}$, which includes the hearing conservation criteria discussed in Chapter 6. The levels in Table 9.6 are only recommended by EPA and do not take into consideration either economic factors or technological problems in arriving at these levels. Local jurisdictions may wish to use these levels for guidance in developing long-range goals, but local conditions may lead to higher or lower values.

An earlier form of the day-night level is the community noise equivalent level (CNEL), which has been adopted by the State of California for environmental noise monitoring purposes. In this case the A-weighted equivalent energy sound level is penalized for evening hours by 5 dB, while nighttime hours are penalized by 10 dB. In this case evening hours are defined between 7 P.M. to 10 P.M., while nighttime hours span from 10 P.M. to 7 A.M. For actual outdoor noise environments, it has been established[2] that L_{dn} is approximately equal to the corresponding CNEL value.

Example 9.5
Given the hourly average sound levels, $L_{eq(1)}$ listed below over a 24-h period, calculate the L_{dn}.

The data are listed in tabular form. The 10-dB penalty has been added to the hourly L_{eq}'s, starting with the 10 P.M. level through the 6 A.M. level.

Time	$L_{eq(1)}$	Adjusted $L_{eq(1)}$	$10^{L_i/10}$ ($\times 10^4$)
Midnight	40	50	10
1	30	40	1
2	30	40	1
3	30	40	1
4	30	40	1
5	30	40	1
6	40	50	10
7	50	50	10
8	60	60	100
9	70	70	1000
10	60	60	100
11	60	60	100
Noon	60	60	100
1	60	60	100
2	60	60	100
3	60	60	100
4	60	60	100
5	70	70	1000
6	60	60	100
7	60	60	100
8	50	50	10
9	50	50	10
10	40	50	10
11	40	50	10
		$\sum_i 10^{L_i/10} =$	3075×10^4

In using Equation 9.1 we observe that $f_i = 1/24$ for each hourly value. Consequently,

$$L_{dn} = 10 \log \left(30.75 \times \frac{10^6}{24} \right)$$
$$= 10 \log(1.28) + 60 = 61.1 \text{ dBA} \qquad \text{Answer}$$

9.7 Noise Pollution Level

The noise pollution level, L_{NP}, is another cumulative rating method that includes both the steady sound present as well as fluctuations in the measured sound. Any annoyance associated with the total energy and the variability of the sound are taken into consideration by this measurement rating scheme. The mathematical definition is:

$$L_{NP} = L_{eq} + 2.56\sigma, \qquad dB(NP) \tag{9.4}$$

in which L_{eq} = energy equivalent sound level of a sufficiently long A-weighted sample of noise in dBA

σ = standard deviation of the same sample in dBA

Note that the units are expressed as dB(NP).

Should the probability distribution of the instantaneous levels be close to a Gaussian distribution, then the L_{10}, L_{50}, and L_{90} levels can be used in Equation 9.4. This leads to the following equation.

$$L_{NP} = L_{eq} + (L_{10} - L_{90})$$
$$= L_{50} + d + \frac{d^2}{60}, \qquad dB(NP) \tag{9.5}$$

in which

$$d = (L_{10} - L_{90}),$$
$$L_{eq} = L_{50} + \frac{d^2}{60}$$

Good correlation has been achieved in England[3] between peoples' level of annoyance from aircraft noise and highway noise with the noise pollution level.

Example 9.6

Assuming that the data in Example 9.1 are Gaussian, find the noise pollution level.

From Example 9.1, $L_{90} = 52.5$ dBA, $L_{50} = 61.7$ dBA, and $L_{10} = 72.5$ dBA. Now,

$$L_{eq} = L_{50} + \frac{d^2}{60}$$
$$= 61.7 + \frac{(72.5 - 52.5)^2}{60}$$
$$= 61.7 + 6.7 = 68.4 \text{ dBA}$$

Therefore,

$$L_{NP} = L_{eq} + (L_{10} - L_{90})$$
$$= 68.4 + 20 = 88.4 \text{ dB(NP)} \qquad \text{Answer}$$

A few comments are in order. First we observe that the above L_{eq} of 68.4 dBA compares favorably with a value of 67.9 dBA that is calculated by the procedure described in Section 9.5. Also we observe that the larger the increment in $(L_{10} - L_{90})$, the greater is the added value to the L_{NP}. This serves as an indicator of peoples' degree of annoyance with their noise environment.

9.8 Measuring for Community Noise

In view of the interest in community noise, equipment manufacturers are developing measurement systems that conveniently provide the statistical levels, L_{eq}, L_{dn}, L_{NP}, and so on. These systems use outdoor microphones that are designed to withstand extreme weather conditions. Some provide a record of the sound level measurements as well as the weather conditions on a tape recorder, while other measurement systems utilize a digital display of the end result, such as the L_{dn}. Automatic time clocks allow the equipment to be left unattended. Because of the large time span during which the sound is being measured, some of the new systems allow the operator to select a sampling time so that the sound is measured for a portion of the time at fixed intervals.

There are other options available to measure community noise. The simplest approach utilizes a hand-held sound level meter, a wind screen, a watch, and a data sheet to record observed levels at a predetermined sampling rate. For example, with the meter set on slow response, A-weighting, suppose we record the levels every 15 s. Whether we select a smaller or larger sampling rate will normally depend on one's endurance, the availability of a partner for recording, and the importance of the measurements. Having the recorded levels every 15 s, say over a 25-min span, we arrange the data in decending order. In this example we have 100 data points, so that the L_{10} corresponds to the tenth highest reading, the L_{50} corresponds to the fiftieth highest reading, and so on. Likewise, a histogram of the data can be constructed by noting the number of times a decibel interval is recorded. This enables us to calculate the L_{eq}, as explained in Section 9.5.

The above describes both sophisticated and relatively simple approaches to measuring community noise levels. Between the two extremes there are other options available. The measuring system one chooses will depend on the frequency of intended use, the budget available, the capabilities of the available personnel, and other special circumstances that will undoubtedly exist.

Example 9.7
Field measurements were made every 15 s over a 25-min span with a sound level meter set on the A-weighting network. The field data are tabulated below. Find the L_{90} and L_{eq} for this case.

By counting the number of readings in decending order, the L_{90} equals 76 dBA, which corresponds to the ninetieth highest reading.

The tabulated data show the fraction of the time each level was observed. For example, there were two readings out of 100 readings at 88 dBA. Consequently, this represents a fraction of 0.02. The remaining columns of data show the usual calculations for finding the L_{eq} equal to 82.3 dBA. It is interesting to note that if 5-dB increments were used starting with 71 to 75 dBA, and if the midpoint values were selected as the average level, an L_{eq} equal to 82.4 dBA would be calculated. This, however, is very close to the more accurate value of 82.3 dBA.

Measured L_p (dBA)	Frequency	f_i	$10^{L_i/10}$ ($\times 10^8$)	$f_i\, 10^{L_i/10}$ ($\times 10^8$)
90	×	0.01	10.00	0.100
89				
88	× ×	0.02	6.31	0.126
87				
86	× × ×	0.03	3.98	0.119
85	× × × × × ×	0.06	3.16	0.190
84	× × × × × × × × ×	0.09	2.51	0.226
83	× × × × × × × × × × × ×	0.12	2.00	0.240
82	× × × × × × × × × × × × × × × × × × ×	0.19	1.58	0.300
81	× × × × × × × × × × × × ×	0.13	1.26	0.164
80	× × × × × × × × ×	0.09	1.00	0.090
79	× × × × × ×	0.06	0.79	0.047
78	× × × × ×	0.05	0.63	0.032
77	× × × ×	0.04	0.50	0.020
76	× ×	0.02	0.40	0.008
75	× × ×	0.03	0.32	0.010
74	× ×	0.02	0.25	0.005
73	×	0.01	0.20	0.002
72	× ×	0.02	0.16	0.003
71	×	0.01	0.13	0.001

$$\sum_I f_i\, 10^{L_i/10} = \overline{1.683 \times 10^8}$$

$$
\begin{aligned}
L_{eq} &= 10 \log 1.683 + 80 \\
&= 2.26 + 80 \\
&= 82.3 \text{ dBA} \qquad \text{Answer}
\end{aligned}
$$

9.9 Summary

A. The important ideas:
   1. Since outdoor community noise levels fluctuate appreciably, statistical indicators are used to describe the noise climate.
   2. The energy equivalent sound level is a measurement of the cumulative exposure to noise over a prescribed time interval.

3. The L_{dn} and CNEL apply decibel penalties during times when people are most sensitive to outdoor noise levels.
4. The L_{eq} and L_{dn} have been adopted by EPA as the units for recommending environmental noise levels so as to protect the public health and welfare with an adequate margin of safety.
5. The L_{10} is used by the Federal Highway Administration in its standards for noise levels from highway operations.
6. The L_{NP} has been proposed in England as a cumulative rating method incorporating the L_{eq} and standard deviation for aircraft noise and highway noise.

B. The important equations:

$$L_{eq} = 10 \log \left(\sum_{i=1}^{n} f_i \, 10^{L_i/10} \right) \tag{9.1}$$

$$L_{eq} = L_1 + 10 \log f_1 \tag{9.3}$$

$$L_{NP} = L_{eq} + 2.56\sigma \tag{9.4}$$

9.10 Assignments

9.1 For the time history of community noise shown in Figure 9.10, (a) construct a histogram using a sampling time of 2 s; (b) calculate the L_{10}, L_{50}, and L_{90} values from the histogram.

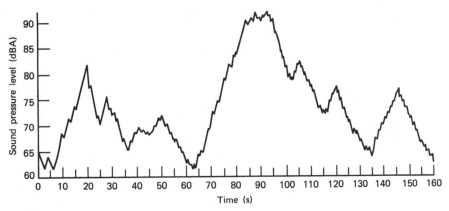

FIGURE 9.10   Problem 9.1.

9.2 Calculate the L_{10}, L_{50}, and L_{90} values for the histogram shown in Figure 9.11.

9.3 Calculate the L_{10}, L_{50}, and L_{90} values for the histogram shown in Figure 9.12.

9.4 Define ambient noise, steady noise, and background noise.

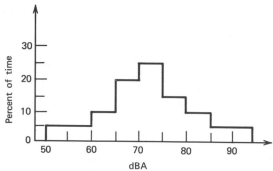

FIGURE 9.11   Problem 9.2.

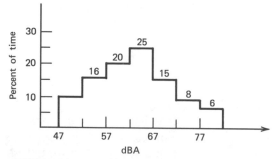

FIGURE 9.12   Problem 9.3.

9.5 Given the following nighttime and daytime equivalent energy sound levels:

$$L_n = 40 \text{ dBA} \qquad \text{(between 10 P.M. to 7 A.M.)}$$
$$L_d = 50 \text{ dBA} \qquad \text{(between 7 A.M. to 10 P.M.)}$$

(a) Find the L_{eq} over the 24-h period.
(b) Find the L_{dn} over the 24-h period.

9.6 Repeat problem 9.5 for $L_n = 68$ dBA and $L_d = 76$ dBA.

9.7 Find the L_{dn} for the following hourly L_{eq}'s.

Time	L_{eq} (dBA)	Time	L_{eq} (dBA)	Time	L_{eq} (dBA)
11 P.M.	50	7	50	3	65
Midnight	40	8	50	4	65
1 A.M.	40	9	50	5	65
2	40	10	65	6	65
3	40	11	65	7	60
4	40	Noon	65	8	60
5	40	1 P.M.	65	9	55
6	40	2	65	10	55

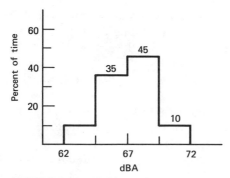

FIGURE 9.13 Problem 9.8.

9.8 Calculate the L_{50} and L_{eq} for the histogram shown in Figure 9.13.
9.9 Calculate the L_{50} and L_{eq} for the histogram shown in Figure 9.14.

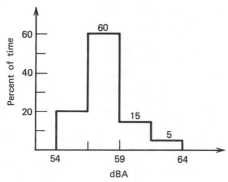

FIGURE 9.14 Problem 9.9.

9.10 How long must a 90-dB source last to have the same L_{eq} as a source of 80 dB that lasts for 1 h?
9.11 An individual's 24-h noise exposure level is shown in Figure 9.15. What is this person's L_{dn} exposure?

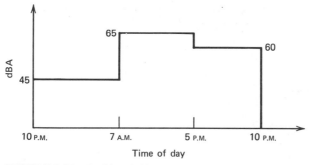

FIGURE 9.15 Problem 9.11.

9.12 During an 8-h period a factory employee is exposed to 81 dBA for the first 2 h, followed by 2 h at 77 dBA. During a 1-h lunch break, the exposure is 66 dBA. For the remaining 3 h, the exposure level is 72 dBA. Calculate the L_{eq} for this 8-h exposure.

9.13 How long may a 105-dBA source be operated daily so as not to exceed an L_{eq} of 60 dBA?

9.14 If the daytime background level is 50 dBA in a community, how long may a source of 85 dBA be operated during daytime hours if the community sets an L_{eq} of 60 dBA for these hours?

9.15 If $L_{eq} = 90$ dBA over an 8-h period, how long may a source of 105 dBA be operated?

9.16 A residential community adopts a 24-h L_{eq} of 55 dBA in its noise ordinance. A siren at the local fire station sounds four times daily on the average, each lasting 15 s. What is the allowable level from the siren under this ordinance if the background level is 52 dBA?

9.17 If $L_1 = 100$ dBA for 4 mins, what is the corresponding L_{eq} for a 15-h period?

9.18 Explain the meaning of Figure 9.8.

9.19 What approach does the L_{NP} take to describe community noise?

9.20 Calculate the noise pollution level for problem 9.2.

9.21 Calculate the noise pollution level for problem 9.3.

9.22 Calculate the noise pollution level for problem 9.8.

9.23 Calculate the noise pollution level for problem 9.9.

9.24 Explain the basis for EPA adopting an $L_{dn} = 55$ dBA as the recommended outdoor level in residential neighborhoods.

9.25 Using a hand-held sound level meter, take dBA readings every 15 s for 30 min on a street corner. Establish the L_{10}, L_{50}, L_{90}, and L_{eq} from the data.

References

[1] L. L. Beranek, *Noise and Vibration Control*, Chapter 4, McGraw-Hill, 1971.

[2] "Information on Levels of Environmental Noise Requisite to Protect Public Health and Welfare with an Adequate Margin of Safety," U.S. Environmental Protection Agency, March 1974.

[3] L. L. Beranek, *Noise and Vibration Control*, Chapter 18, McGraw-Hill, 1971.

10
TRANSPORTATION NOISE

Until now we have been studying community noise levels from all sound sources, both near and far. In the day-night average sound levels we include transportation noise sources along with any other noise sources in the community. Because of the significant impact of jet aircraft noise on our environment, particularly on those communities bordering on airports, special noise rating schemes have been developed that are intended to correlate jet aircraft noise levels with human response. Noise generated from highways and railroads are also important noise sources that contribute significantly to environmental noise pollution. In this chapter we shall examine the methods for predicting the impact that these major sources have on the noise climate of a community.

10.1 Growth of Transportation Noise

Since the early 1950s, the number of transportation aircraft and surface vehicles has increased tremendously. Table 10.1 lists the growth of different surface vehicles and aircraft in the United States. While passenger cars, trucks, buses, and highway vehicles grew appreciably from 1950 to 1970, it is noteworthy that off-road motorcycles and snowmobiles are of recent origin. These recreation vehicles have frequently created citizen protest due to the high noise levels that they generate. We also observe from Table 10.1 that the jet aircraft was introduced during this period, along with a tremendous rise in both general aviation aircraft and helicopters.

Rising environmental noise levels have accompanied this growth in the transportation industry, as indicated in Table 10.2. We observe that the number of square miles of land having a CNEL greater than 65 dB has risen sharply because of airports and freeways. At this CNEL level, widespread

TABLE 10.1
Growth in the Transporation System, 1950–1970

Source	1950	1960	1970
Population (in millions)	151	181	204
Passenger cars (in millions)	40.4	61.7	87.0
Trucks and buses (in millions)	8.8	12.2	19.3
Motorcycles (in millions) (highway)	0.45	0.51	1.2
Motorcycles (in millions) (off-road)	—	—	1.8
Snowmobiles (in millions)	0	0.002	1.6
2-3 engine turbofan aircraft	0	0	1174
4-engine turbofan aircraft	0	202	815
General aviation aircraft	45,000	76,200	136,000
Helicopters	85	634	2800

Source. "Transportation Noise and Noise from Equipment Powered by Internal Combustion Engines," EPA, NTID 300.13, December 1971.

TABLE 10.2
Summary of Estimated Noise Impacted Land (Within CNEL 65 Contour) Near Airports and Freeways from 1955–1970

	Impacted Land Area—Square Miles		
	Near Airports	Near Freeways	Total
1955	~20	8	28
1960	200	75	275
1965	760	285	1045
1970	1450	545	1995

Source. "Transportation Noise and Noise from Equipment Powered by Internal Combustion Engines," NTID 300.13, December 1971.

complaints are to be expected from the estimated 10 million people living in these noise-impacted areas. These land areas will continue to grow unless federal, state, and local agencies introduce enforceable regulatory action to control the noise levels generated by these major noise sources. We shall examine this aspect of controlling noise in Chapter 12.

In addition to the impact of transportation noise on communities, Table 10.3 shows the potential hearing damage from transportation vehicles as experienced by vehicle occupants. This analysis, made in 1971, assumes

TABLE 10.3
Average-to-maximum Equivalent 8-h Exposure Level for a Variety of Transportation Vehicles

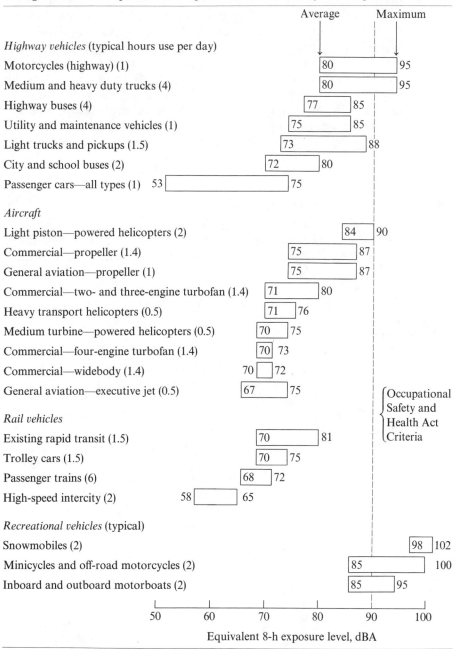

Source. "Transportation Noise and Noise Equipment Powered by Internal Combustion Engines," EPA, NTID 300.13, December 1971.

the typical number of hours of use on a given day and correlates the noise level exposure to an equivalent 8-h exposure. This correlation uses an 8-h exposure at 90 dBA as being equivalent to 4 h at 95 dBA, 2 h at 100 dBA, 1 h at 105 dBA, 1/2 h at 110 dBA, and 1/4 h at 115 dBA. This scheme follows the allowable occupational noise levels prescribed by the Occupational Safety and Health Administration, as we shall see in Chapter 11. For example, a person who rides a motorcycle 1 h each day receives an equivalent 8-h exposure ranging from an average of 80 dBA to a maximum of 95 dBA. We observe from the list in Table 10.3 that unprotected ears of users of recreational vehicles are receiving very high equivalent 8-h exposure levels. If this occurs on a regular basis, a noise-induced permanent threshold shift in hearing is likely to occur.

10.2 Perceived Noise Level

We have observed in Table 10.3 the range of indoor noise levels in terms of equivalent 8-h exposure levels for various types of aircraft. The comfort of the passenger has been carefully considered in the design of most aircraft, particularly for the commercial jet aircraft. We now turn our attention to the plight of the innocent bystander living in the vicinity of the aircraft flight path. To do this, we shall examine some rating methods that have been developed to measure the bystander's level of annoyance from this airborne noise.

The perceived noise level (PNL) is a calculated single number based on known levels of people's annoyance from fixed-wing jet aircraft flyover noise. Karl Kryter[1] developed this approach by examining the time duration and spectral complexity of the noise. The set of equal noisiness contours shown in Figure 10.1 was developed from this investigation and form the basis for calculating the PNL, as described below.

Field measurements are made during an aircraft flyover event using 1/1 or 1/3 octave band recordings with a real time analyzer and digital computer. Discrete sets of data are recorded in increments no larger than 0.5 s. For each set of data the following calculations are made by the computer.

1. Convert the octave band data to noys using Figure 10.1.
2. Calculate the effective noy value N_t as follows:

$$N_t = 0.3 \sum_i N_i + 0.7\, N_{max} \quad (1/1 \text{ octave band data}) \qquad (10.1)$$

$$N_t = 0.15 \sum_i N_i + 0.85\, N_{max} \quad (1/3 \text{ octave band data}) \qquad (10.2)$$

3. The chart in Figure 10.1 converts the N_t value to the equivalent perceived noise level, which is expressed in units of PNdB.

The above method is widely used in current evaluations of the annoyance effect experienced from aircraft flyovers. Currently, the Federal Aviation

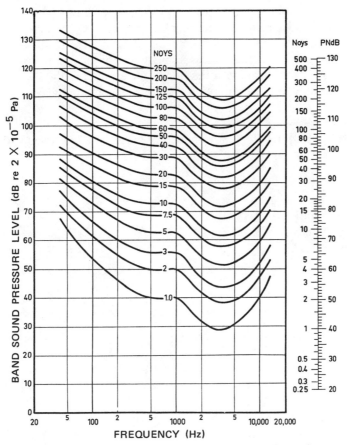

FIGURE 10.1   Equal noisiness contours. (Source. J. T. Broch, Acoustic Noise Measurements, B & K Instruments, Inc., January 1971.)

Administration (FAA) certifies certain size jet aircraft in terms of the PNL in its regulations. Keep in mind that the noy contours have been developed for aircraft noise effects only and should not necessarily be extended to other forms of environmental noise.

Recently, the D-weighting network has been suggested as an approximation for measuring PNL. While it has not been officially adopted by any international standards organization, some of the newer sound level meters contain this weighting network (which is, in fact, the inverted 40-noy contour of equal annoyance). A reading on the D-weighting network for an aircraft flyover is represented as L_D, so that the PNL is found approximately as follows:

$$PNL = L_D + 7, \quad PNdB \tag{10.3}$$

10.2 PERCEIVED NOISE LEVEL   **155**

The PNL is useful as a measure of a single flyover of a jet aircraft. For example, John F. Kennedy International Airport in New York limits ground levels to 112 PNdB at selected monitoring stations close to the end of the runways. Also, it is the basic measurement used in cumulative-type noise rating methods that have been developed for evaluating the overall noise impact from fixed-wing jet aircraft operations on communities.

Example 10.1
Calculate the PNL for the following octave band data associated with a jet aircraft.

i	f_c (Hz)	L_p (dB)	N_i (noys)
1	63	90	15
2	125	102	45
3	250	105	75
4	500	100	65
5	1000	92	38
6	2000	87	45
7	4000	81	37
8	8000	70	12
		$\sum_{i=1}^{8} N_i = 332$	

The data are arranged in tabular form in the first three columns. Column 4 lists the converted octave band levels in noys. Referring to Equation 10.1,

$$N_t = 0.3(332) + 0.7(75)$$
$$= 152.1 \text{ noys}$$

The chart in Figure 10.1 converts this value to a PNL value of 113 PNdB.

10.3 Composite Noise Rating for Aircraft Noise

The composite noise rating (CNR) for fixed-wing aircraft noise was introduced[2] in 1957 to evaluate the noise impact of military aircraft operations on neighboring communities. Later modifications of the method were made to include commercial jet aircraft. The CNR method develops contours based on daily aircraft operations around an airport that are, in effect, equal noise level exposures using the PNL in PNdB, the number of daytime and nighttime flight operations, and a 10 dB nighttime penalty. In developing these contours the aircraft are grouped into classes according to type, engine size, and performance.

TABLE 10.4

CNR Levels for Takeoffs, Landings, and Ground Runups and the Expected Community Response

Takeoffs and Landings	Ground Runups	Zone	Description of Expected Response
Less than 100	Less than 80	1	Essentially no complaints expected.
100 to 115	80 to 95	2	Individuals may complain, perhaps vigorously. Concerted group action is possible.
Greater than 115	>95	3	Individual reactions would likely include repeated vigorous complaints. Concerted group action might be expected.

The CNR contours are superimposed on a map of the airport area, providing noise exposures at a given location for three separate operations: takeoff, landing, and ground runups. Table 10.4 shows the CNR levels, zones, and a description of the expected response from people living in the designated area.

While these CNR contours have not been endorsed by the civil aviation community, they are widely used to evaluate the noise impact from military flight operations on communities near the airports. Having such information available, a land developer could recommend different types of zoning based upon the CNR contours. Those areas in the high noise levels should be zoned for industrial use, followed by commercial use and residential use.

10.4 Noise Exposure Forecast

The noise exposure forecast (NEF) was introduced in 1964 for commercial jet aircraft as an extension and updating of the CNR for civil aircraft noise.[3] The development of the NEF contours closely follows the CNR approach. In this case we introduce the single event effective perceived noise level (EPNL) in EPNdB as follows.

$$EPNL = PNL_{max} + D + F, \qquad EPNdB \qquad (10.4)$$

in which PNL_{max} = maximum perceived noise level during flyover of a single aircraft

$D = 10 \log(\Delta t/20)$, where Δt is the time interval in seconds during which the noise level is within 10 PNdB of the maximum PNL

F = correction for the presence of discrete frequency components (usually about 3 dB)

Figure 10.2 shows graphically how Δt is obtained.

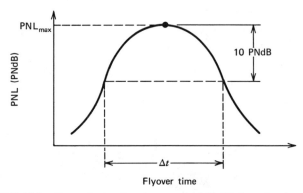

FIGURE 10.2   Example showing the measured 10-dB downtime Δt.

Further details in developing NEF contour values are provided[4] by identifying the class of aircraft with the subscript i and the flight path by j. Representing the general case by EPNL_{ij} for some designated point on the ground, and knowing the corresponding number of daytime flights, $n_D(ij)$, and nighttime flights, $n_N(ij)$, the NEF for this type aircraft i using flight path j is :

$$\text{NEF}_{ij} = \text{EPNL}_{ij} + 10 \log \left[\frac{n_D(ij)}{K_D} + \frac{n_N(ij)}{K_N} \right] - C \qquad (10.5)$$

The values of the constants $K_D = 20$ and $K_N = 1.2$ signify that a single nighttime flight contributes to the NEF calculation as much as 17 daytime flights. The value of $C = 75$ is arbitrarily chosen so as to avoid confusion with other existing composite noise rating methods.

Finally, summing for all classes of aircraft using a particular airport and including all possible flight paths, we obtain the NEF value at the designated point of interest.

$$\text{NEF} = 10 \log \left(\sum_i \sum_j 10^{NEF_{ij}/10} \right) \qquad (10.6)$$

We note the similarity between this equation and Equation 9.1 used for calculating the L_{eq}. In both cases we are summing the sound energy present in the environment. Since the L_{dn} is a 24-h L_{eq} with a 10 dB nighttime penalty, it is not too surprising that the following relationship has been shown to exist.[5]

$$L_{dn} = (\text{NEF} + 35) \pm 3 \text{ dBA} \qquad (10.7)$$

There are computer programs for the digital computer that generate NEF contours around a given airport. A sample of the contours is shown in Figure 10.3. Such contours are now available for many major airports around

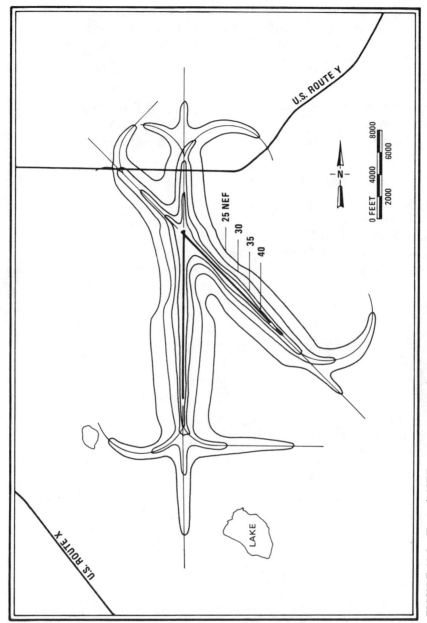

FIGURE 10.3 Typical NEF contours around an airport. (Source. "Transportation Noise and its Control," U.S. Dept. of Transportation, June 1972.)

the country. The contours have been used by the Federal Housing and Urban Development Agency (HUD) in evaluating land uses around airports[6] and are normally included in environmental impact statements dealing with noise from fixed-wing jet aircraft operations around airport communities.

10.5 Approximate Construction of NEF Contours

The following is a guide for constructing approximate NEF contours as prescribed by HUD.[7] In this procedure we first calculate the airport traffic index.

$$\text{airport traffic index} = X = N_d + 17\,N_n \tag{10.8}$$

in which N_d, N_n = number of jet operations (takeoffs plus landings) during daytime and nighttime at the airport, respectively

Having X, refer to Table 10.5 and Figure 10.4 to construct the approximate NEF-30 and NEF-40 contours for each runway at a given airport. Having constructed the NEF-30 and -40 contours on a scaled map, locate a point

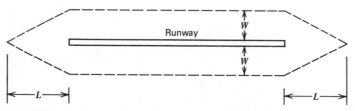

FIGURE 10.4 *Approximate construction of the NEF contours in which L and W are prescribed in Table 10.5.*

TABLE 10.5
Recommended L/W Ratios for Approximate Construction of NEF Contours for Airport Traffic Indices

	Contour Size	
	NEF-30	NEF-40
X	L/W	L/W
50	1 mi/0.5 mi	none
50–500	3 mi/0.5 mi	1 mi/1000 ft
500–1300	6 mi/1.5 mi	2.5 mi/2000 ft
1300	10 mi/2 mi	4 mi/3000 ft

Source. "Noise Assessment Guidelines," U.S. Dept. of Housing and Urban Development, August 1971.

TABLE 10.6
Site Exposure to Aircraft Noise

Distance from Site to the Center of the Area Covered by the Principal Runways	Acceptability Category
Outside the NEF-30 (CNR-100) contour, at a distance greater than or equal to the distance between the NEF-30 and NEF-40 (CNR-100, CNR-115) contours	Clearly acceptable
Outside the NEF-30 (CNR-100) contour, at a distance less than the distance between the NEF-30 and NEF-40 (CNR-100, CNR-115) contours	Normally acceptable
Between the NEF-30 and NEF-40 (CNR-100, CNR-115) contours	Normally unacceptable
Within the NEF-40 (CNR-115) contour	Clearly unacceptable

Source. Noise Assessment Guidelines, U.S. Dept. of Housing and Urban Development, 1971.

roughly in the center of the area covered by the principal runways. If the site in question lies outside the NEF-30 contour, construct a straight line between the center point and the site point on the map. Finally, refer to Table 10.6 to establish HUD's acceptability category of the site for possible housing construction.

Example 10.2
An airport has 150 daytime and 30 nighttime jet aircraft operations. Referring to Figure 10.5, evaluate sites number 1 and 2 according to the HUD criteria.

First calculate the airport traffic index using Equation 10.8.

$$X = N_d + 17 N_n$$
$$= 150 + 17(30) = 660$$

From Table 10.5,

$$\frac{L}{W} = 6 \text{ mi}/1.5 \text{ mi}, \qquad \text{NEF-30 contour}$$

$$\frac{L}{W} = 2.5 \text{ mi}/2000 \text{ ft}, \qquad \text{NEF-40 contour}$$

The approximate NEF contours are shown as dashed lines in Figure 10.5. Site number 1 lies outside the NEF-30 contour at a distance greater than the distance between the NEF-30 and NEF-40 contours. This site is "clearly acceptable" by the HUD criteria shown in Table 10.6. Site number 2 also lies outside the NEF-30 contour, but at a distance less than the distance between the NEF-30 and NEF-40 contours. This site is rated "normally acceptable,"

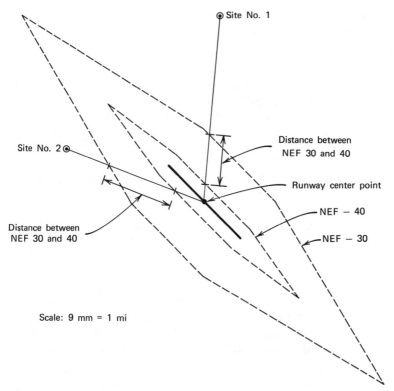

FIGURE 10.5 *Construction of the NEF contours in Example 10.2.*

which means that a building located at site number 2 must include acoustical construction measures to attenuate the interior noise from the airport operations.

10.6 Highway Noise

The noise generated from highway traffic is another major source of environmental noise pollution. To begin our examination of highway noise, let us consider the noise characteristics of motor vehicles shown in Figure 10.6.[8] Here we observe the generalized octave band noise spectra for diesel trucks and passenger cars at a 50-ft (15.2 m) distance. The curve for the diesel trucks is the mean spectra for 26 trucks tested on a level roadway. Large variations from this energy distribution occur for other operating conditions, such as acceleration, upgrade and downgrade motion, turning, and so on. Likewise, individual differences exist among trucks because of different diesel engines, type of brakes, condition of tires, and special individual equipment. The generalized octave band noise spectrum for passenger cars shown in Figure

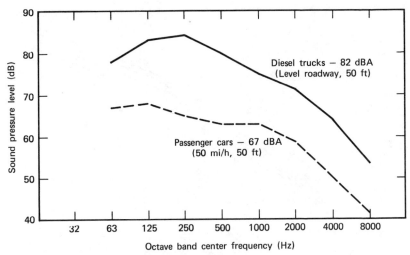

FIGURE 10.6   Generalized noise spectra for diesel trucks and passenger cars at 50-ft distance. (*Source. W. J. Galloway, W. E. Clark, and J. S. Kerrick, "Highway Noise Measurements, Simulation, and Mixed Reactions," NCHRP Report 78, 1969.*)

10.6 is derived from data taken on 133 passenger cars. Analysis of the data showed that the frequency spectrum shape for the cars exhibited no important changes over a speed range from 30 mi/h (48.3 km/h) to 65 mi/h (104.6 km/h).

Empirical relationships have been developed that predict both the L_{50} and L_{10} levels for freely flowing highway traffic. The relationship for passenger cars shows the L_{50} being proportional to the traffic density measured in vehicles per mile, the cube of the vehicle speed measured in miles per hour, and inversely proportional to the distance from the roadway centerline measured in feet. Since the traffic density (vehicles per mile) equals the vehicle volume (vehicles per hour) divided by vehicle speed, the relationship for predicting the L_{50} may include the vehicle volume instead of the traffic density. Figure 10.7 shows the results in graphical form for the case where the distance equals 100 ft (30.5 m) from the traffic traveling on a single lane. We observe that as average traffic speed increases for a given automobile volume, the sound pressure level increases, as one would intuitively expect.

In predicting the noise generated by diesel trucks, the empirical relationship shows that the L_{50} is proportional to the vehicle density only, and inversely proportional to the distance from the roadway centerline. Replacing the vehicle density by the vehicle volume divided by the vehicle speed, we obtain the graphical results shown in Figure 10.8. Here we observe that as the truck speed increases at a fixed vehicle volume, the predicted sound pressure level decreases. This unexpected result is because the L_{50} is now

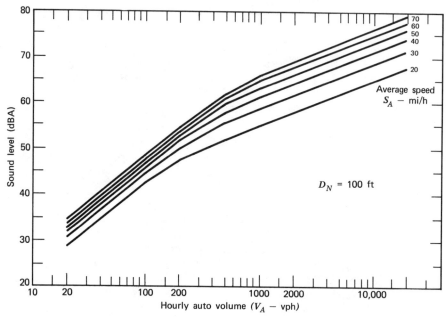

FIGURE 10.7 Sound pressure level as a function of hourly auto volume for average speeds, reference distance of 100 ft. (Source. C. G. Gordon, W. J. Galloway, B. A. Kugler, and D. L. Nelson "Highway Noise—A Design Guide for Highway Engineers," NCHRP Report 117, 1971.)

proportional to the vehicle volume and inversely proportional to the vehicle speed and distance to the roadway. As in the case of Figure 10.7, the set of curves in Figure 10.8 is for the trucks traveling in a single lane and the distance is 100 ft (30.5 m) from the roadway centerline.

10.7 Procedure for Predicting Highway Noise

The procedure[9] for predicting the noise generated from freely flowing highway traffic requires that the contribution from automobiles be made separately from diesel trucks. The two results are then added to obtain the combined predicted values. The following outlines the procedures to calculate the L_{50} and L_{10} levels for highway traffic flowing along a straight, infinitely long roadway lying at grade on a flat level terrain.

    1. Calculation of the L_{50} level.

        a. Establish the volume flow, V, for automobiles in vehicles per hour and the volume flow for heavy trucks in vehicles per hour.

        b. Establish the average speed, S, of each vehicle class in miles per hour.

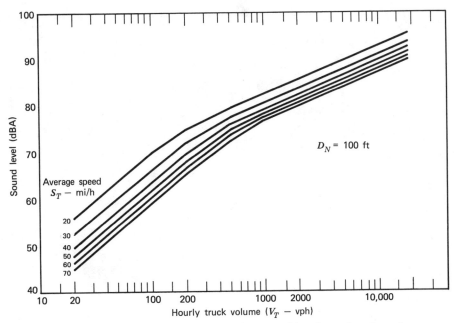

FIGURE 10.8   Sound pressure level as a function of hourly truck volume for average speeds, reference distance of 100 ft. (Source. C. G. Gordon, W. J. Galloway, B. A. Kugler, and D. L. Nelson, "Highway Noise—A Design Guide for Highway Engineers," NCHRP Report 117, 1971.)

    c. Use Figures 10.7 and 10.8 to find the reference L_{50} levels for each vehicle class, respectively.

    d. Use Figure 10.9 to correct the levels in step c to account for roadway width (or number of lanes) and observation distance from the nearest lane centerline, D_N in feet.

    e. Add logarithmically the corrected results of step d to obtain the final L_{50} value.

2. Calculation of the L_{10} level.

    a. Compute the single-lane equivalent distance D_E using

$$D_E = \sqrt{D_N D_F} \tag{10.9}$$

in which D_N and D_F are the nearest and farthest distances from lane centerlines to the observation point, respectively, measured in feet.

    b. For each vehicle class, calculate VD_E/S and enter Figure 10.10 to obtain $(L_{10} - L_{50})$, in which L_{50} is the level found in procedure 1 above. This establishes the L_{10} for each vehicle class.

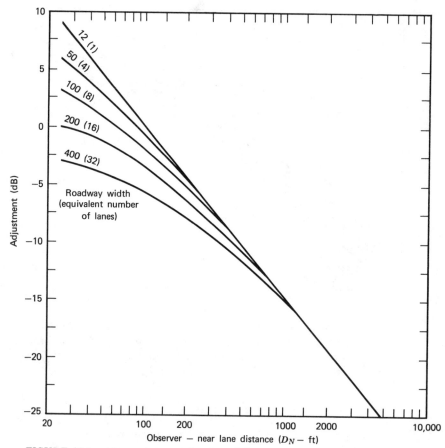

FIGURE 10.9 *Attenuation as a function of the near lane distance to the observer for different roadway widths (equivalent number of lanes). (Source. C. G. Gordon, W. J. Galloway, B. A. Kugler, and D. L. Nelson, "Highway Noise—A Design Guide for Highway Engineers," NCHRP Report 117, 1971.)*

    c. Add logarithmically the results of step b to obtain the final L_{10} value.

Adjustments to these L_{50} and L_{10} levels can be made to account for curves, gradients, cross-sectional changes, nonlevel terrain, and junctions. Details of these steps are found in reference 9.

Example 10.3

A six-lane highway has 8000 automobiles per hour traveling at an average speed of 55 mi/h (88.5 km/h). The truck volume is 150 per hour traveling at an average speed of 50 mi/h (80.5 km/h). Predict the L_{50} and L_{10} levels 150 ft

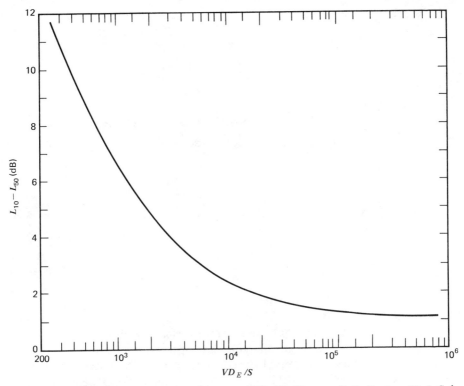

FIGURE 10.10 $L_{10}-L_{50}$ *as a function of* VD_E/S. *(Source. C. G. Gordon, W. J. Gal-loway, B. A. Kugler, and D. L. Nelson, "Highway Noise—A Design Guide for Highway Engineers," NCHRP Report 117, 1971.)*

(45.7 m) from the centerline of the nearest lane from this traffic flow. Let the centerline distance to the farthest lane equal 350 ft (106.7 m). Assume level terrain, straight flow, and so on.

1. Calculation of the L_{50} level.

    a. $V_A = 8000$ vph, $V_T = 150$ vph.

    b. $S_A = 55$ mi/h, $S_T = 50$ mi/h.

    c. From Figure 10.7, $L_{50} = 72.5$ dBA for automobiles.
       From Figure 10.8, $L_{50} = 65$ dBA for trucks.

    d. Since $D_N = 150$ ft, Figure 10.9 calls for an adjustment of -3 dB for a six-lane highway. Therefore,

$$L_{50} = 69.5 \text{ dBA for automobiles}$$

$$L_{50} = 62 \text{ dBA for trucks}$$

    e. Adding logarithmically 69.5 dBA to 62 dBA, we obtain a final value of $L_{50} = 70.2$ dBA   Answer

2. Calculation of the L_{10} level.

   a. $D_E = \sqrt{D_N D_F} = \sqrt{150(350)} = \sqrt{52500} = 229 \, ft.$

   b. For automobiles, $V_A D_E / S_A = 8000(229)/55 = 33{,}300.$
      For trucks, $V_T D_E / S_T = 150(229)/50 = 687.$
      Using Figure 10.10, $(L_{10} - L_{50}) = 1.6$, for automobiles.

    Therefore,

$$L_{10} = 69.5 + 1.6 = 71.1 \text{ dBA for automobiles}$$

$$(L_{10} - L_{50}) = 7.7, \text{ for trucks}$$

    Therefore,

$$L_{10} = 62 + 7.7 = 69.7 \text{ dBA for trucks}$$

   c. Adding logarithmically 71.1 dBA to 69.7 dBA, we obtain a final value of

$$L_{10} = 73.5 \text{ dBA} \qquad \text{Answer}$$

10.8 Railroad Line Noise

Recent investigations[10,11,12] on the cumulative noise from railroad line operations enable us to approximate the impact from this intrusive noise in terms of L_{dn}. The noise generated by line operations consists of two major sources: the noise generated by the locomotive and the noise generated by the passing cars. Figure 10.11 shows the variation of the A-weighted sound pressure level as a function of the time duration. Analysis of field measurements shows that the locomotive noise does not vary appreciably with speed, while car noise is directly related to both the train speed (the faster the speed

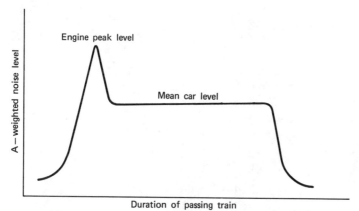

FIGURE 10.11 *Typical noise generated by a passing train showing the engine peak level followed by the mean car noise level.*

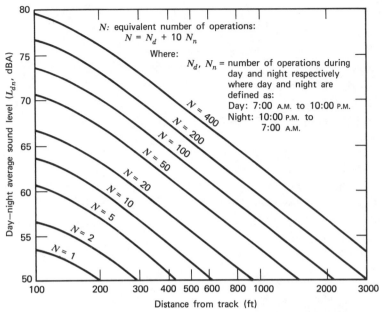

FIGURE 10.12 *Relationship between* L_{dn}, *distance from track, and equivalent number of daily operations.* (*Source. J. Swing, "Railroad Noise," Sound and Vibration, Vol. 9, No. 2, February 1975.*)

the higher the noise) and the train bypass time (the longer the bypass time the higher the noise exposure). Since faster trains have lower bypass times, the two components of the car noise tend to compensate each other. Consequently, the train speed is omitted in predicting railroad line noise.

In addition to the distance from the track centerline to the point in question, the number of daytime operations, N_D, and the number of nighttime operations, N_N, are required information for predicting the L_{dn} from the railroad line operations. In arriving at N_D and N_N, these numbers may be based on the mean daily level of activity over a normal work week. Seasonal variations can be included by dividing the total yearly activity by 365 in arriving at N_D and N_N.

Having established N_D and N_N, the equivalent number of operations, N, is calculated as follows.

$$N = N_D + 10 N_N \tag{10.10}$$

Having N, enter Figure 10.12 at the prescribed distance and proceed vertically to the appropriate N contour. Move across horizontally to read the predicted L_{dn}. If necessary, use Table 10.7 to account for the variables listed. In the case of multiple occurrences of these variables, only the larger of the adjustment values should be used.

Table 10.7
Adjustments to L_{dn} Noise Contours

Variables Affecting Noise Output	Corrections to Desired L_{dn} Value (dB)
1. Passenger trains only (if combination of passenger and freight—assume all freight)	−1
2. Presence of helper engines:	
a. Level grade or descending grade	0
b. Ascending grade	+2
3. Mainline welded or jointed track	0
4. Low-speed classified jointed track	+4
5. Presence of switching frogs or grade crossings	+4
6. Tight radius curve	
a. Radius less than 600 ft	+4
b. Radius 600 to 900 ft	+0.5
c. Radius greater than 900 ft	0
7. Presence of bridgework	
a. Light steel trestle	+14
b. Heavy steel trestle	+5
c. Concrete structure	0

Source. J. W. Swing, "Simplified Procedure for Developing Railroad Noise Exposure Contours," *Sound and Vibration*, February 1975, p. 22.

Example 10.4
Calculate the predicted L_{dn} at a distance of 200 ft (61.0 m) from a track centerline for the following typical 24-h train operations:

Type	Direction	N_D	N_N
Freight	Northbound	8	5
Passenger	Northbound	7	3
Freight	Southbound	9	5
Passenger	Southbound	6	4
	Total	30	17

The equivalent number of operations is obtained using Equation 10.10.

$$N = N_D + 10\,N_N$$
$$= 30 + 10(17) = 200$$

Entering Figure 10.12, we obtain $L_{dn} = 72.5$ dBA at 200 ft (61.0 m) from the track centerline.

10.9 Summary

A. The important ideas:

1. With the rapid growth of transportation vehicles since 1950, there has been a significant increase in community noise levels.
2. Recreation vehicles pose a potential hearing hazard to the users who do not wear ear protection devices.
3. The perceived noise level calculation employs equal noisiness contours, similar to the loudness contours discussed in Chapter 6.
4. The noise exposure forecast includes the effective perceived noise level and the number of daytime and nighttime flights, where it is assumed that one nighttime flight contributes as much as 17 daytime flights.
5. Noise levels from freeways are calculated in terms of the L_{50} and L_{10}, knowing the volume flow, average speed, and roadway width.
6. Approximate L_{dn} contours can be generated for railroad line operations.

B. The important equations:

1. $N_t = 0.3 \sum_i N_i + 0.7 N_{max}$ (1/1 octave band data)   (10.1)

2. $N_t = 0.15 \sum_i N_i + 0.85 N_{max}$ (1/3 octave band data)   (10.2)

3. $\text{PNL} = L_D + 7$ (10.3)

4. $\text{EPNL} = \text{PNL}_{max} + D + F$ (10.4)

5. $\text{NEF} = 10 \log \left(\sum_i \sum_j 10^{\text{NEF}_{ij}/10} \right)$ (10.6)

6. $L_{dn} = (\text{NEF} + 35) \pm 3$ dB   (10.7)

10.10 Assignments

10.1 Discuss the per capita changes in surface transportation vehicles from 1950 to 1970 in the United States.

10.2 Plot the number of aircraft in 1950, 1960, and 1970. Include separate curves for turbofan aircraft, general aviation aircraft, and helicopters.

10.3 What is the percentage increase from 1955 to 1970 in the impacted land area within the CNEL 65 contour from airport and freeway noise?

10.4 List those vehicles that expose the users to levels in excess of the recommended 8-h levels of the OSHA criteria.

10.5 Calculate the PNL for the following octave band data.

f_c(Hz)	63	125	250	500	1000	2000	4000	8000
L_p(dB)	83	88	88	94	98	95	88	68

10.6 Calculate the PNL for the following octave band data.

f_c(Hz)	63	125	250	500	1000	2000	4000	8000
L_p(dB)	98	100	93	88	84	90	92	75

10.7 A sound level meter equipped with the D-weighting network records a maximum level of 104 dBD during a jet aircraft flyover. What is the approximate PNL?

10.8 What are the major differences between the CNR and NEF rating methods?

10.9 Calculate the EPNL for the data shown in Figure 10.13 assuming $F = 3$ dB.

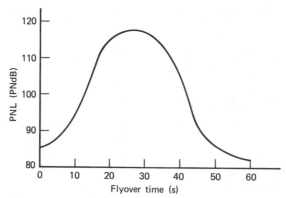

FIGURE 10.13   Problem 10.9.

10.10 The following data are compiled for aircraft operations around an airport at a specified location:

i	j	NEF_{ij}
1	1	28
1	2	30
2	1	29
2	2	32
3	1	30
3	2	34

Calculate the NEF value at this location. Express this result in L_{dn}.

10.11 A runway at an airport is 1 mi long and has the following average daily jet traffic: $N_d = 150$, $N_n = 30$. Construct the approximate NEF 30 and 40 contours for this runway.

10.12 For the two runways shown in Figure 10.14, evaluate sites number 1 and 2 by the HUD criteria. Assume $N_d = 120$, $N_n = 20$ for each runway.

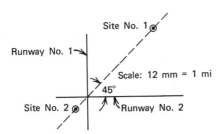

FIGURE 10.14   Problem 10.12.

10.13 For the two runways shown in Figure 10.15, evaluate sites number 1 and 2 by the HUD criteria. Assume $N_d = 200$, $N_n = 40$ for each runway.

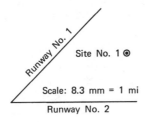

FIGURE 10.15   Problem 10.13.

10.14 What are the limitations of the highway prediction method for the L_{50} levels as outlined in this chapter?

10.15 A four-lane freeway has 3000 automobiles per hour traveling at 60 mi/h (96.5 km/h) average speed. What is the L_{50} experienced by an observer 200 ft (61.0 m) from the nearest lane? Assume flat terrain, and so on.

10.16 For the highway in problem 10.15, 200 trucks per hour travel at 50 mi/h (80.5 km/h) average speed. What is the L_{50} contribution from the trucks at the observer site?

10.17 An eight-lane expressway has 8000 automobiles per hour at 65 mi/h (104.6 km/h) and 200 trucks per hour at 60 mi/h (96.5 km/h) during the peak traffic flow of the day. What is the L_{50} and L_{10} for an observer located 300 ft (91.4 m) from the nearest lane, assuming a farthest lane distance of 450 ft (137.2 m)?

10.18 Calculate the predicted L_{dn} at distances of 500 ft (152.4 m) and 1000 ft (304.8 m) from a track centerline for the following typical 24-h train operations:

Type	Direction	N_D	N_N
Freight	Eastbound	10	6
Passenger	Eastbound	6	2
Freight	Westbound	12	7
Passenger	Westbound	6	2

10.19 Develop the L_{dn} levels for the train operations in problem 10.18, assuming the presence of a grade crossing.

References

[1] K. D. Kryter, "Scaling Human Reactions to the Sound from Aircraft," *J. Acoust. Soc. Am.* 31, pp. 1415–1429, 1959.

[2] K. N. Stevens, A. C. Pietrasanta, and the Staff of Bolt, Beranek and Newman, Inc., "Procedures for Estimating Noise Exposure and Resulting Community Reactions from Air Base Operations," WADC TN-57-10, Wright-Patterson Air Force Base, Ohio, 1957.

[3] D. E. Bishop and R. D. Horonjeff, "Procedure for Developing Noise Exposure Forecast Areas for Aircraft Flight Operations," FAA Report DS 67-10, Washington, D.C., August 1967.

[4] L. L. Beranek, *Noise and Vibration Control*, Chapter 18, McGraw-Hill, 1971.

[5] "Information on Levels of Environmental Noise Requisite to Protect Public Health and Welfare with an Adequate Margin of Safety," U.S. Environmental Protection Agency, Appendix A, March 1974.

[6] "Circular Policy No. 1390.2, "U.S. Housing and Urban Development Agency, August 1971.

[7] T. J. Schultz and N. M. McMahon, "Noise Assessment Guidlines," U.S. Dept. of Housing and Urban Development, August 1971.

[8] "Highway Noise—Measurement, Simulation, and Mixed Reactions," National Cooperative Highway Research Program Report 78, Highway Research Board, National Academy of Sciences—National Academy of Engineering, 1969.

[9] "Highway Noise—A Design Guide for Highway Engineers," National Cooperative Highway Research Program Report 117, Highway Research Board, National Academy of Sciences—National Academy of Engineering, 1971.

[10] J. W. Swing and D. B. Pies' "Assessment of Noise Environments Around Railroad Operations," Wyle Laboratories, Report WCR 73-5, July 1973.

[11] J. W. Swing and D. J. Inman, "Noise Levels in Railroad Operations," A.S.M.E. Rail Transportation Division, No. 74-WA/RT-8, November 1974.

[12] J. W. Swing, "Simplified Procedure for Developing Railroad Noise Exposure Contours," *Sound and Vibration*, February 1975.

11
INDUSTRIAL NOISE

Audiologists have studied the correlation between indoor industrial noise levels and hearing impairment of industrial workers. These investigations enabled the U.S. Congress to amend the Walsh-Healey Public Contracts Act in 1969 to include, for the first time, allowable occupational noise levels. These occupational noise levels were included in the Occupational Safety and Health Act of 1970 to cover the industries engaged in interstate commerce. Both of these laws have generated a great deal of interest in noise control techniques by many industries subject to this new far-reaching legislation.

In our treatment of industrial noise we shall consider both the indoor and the outdoor noise environment. Although most of the data collected on industrial noise is for indoor steady-state noise exposure, there is growing interest in the noise levels reaching the surrounding communities from industrial operations, particularly outdoor construction activities.

11.1 Outdoor Industrial Noise

Whether we are viewing industrial noise as contributing to the indoor or the outdoor environment, the major sources of plant noise[1] may include electromechanical machines (motors, generators, etc.), combustion processes (furnaces), fluid motion (fans, compressors), impact machines (punching, hammers, stamping), and unbalanced or improperly fitted mechanical parts (shafts, gears). Most plants contain only portions of these noise sources and, for many, their noise problem is strictly limited to the indoors.

Plant sites are generally located close to urban communities in order to draw on a ready supply of skilled and semiskilled workers. Because of this close proximity, outdoor industrial operations may produce noise levels that create unhappy neighbors, particularly for those who do not work at the plant. In recent years many companies have moved their industrial operations

TABLE 11.1
**Typical Sound Levels at 50 ft and Total Sound Energy Emitted by
Major Construction Equipment**

Construction Equipment	Typical Sound Level (dBA at 50 ft)	Estimated Total Sound Power (kw-hr/day)
Dump truck	88	296
Portable air compressor	81	147
Concrete mixer (truck)	85	111
Jackhammer	88	84
Scraper	88	79
Dozer	87	78
Paver	89	75
Generator	76	65
Piledriver	101	62
Rock drill	98	53
Pump	76	47
Pneumatic tools	85	36
Backhoe	85	33

Source. Federal Register, Vol. 39, No. 121, pp. 22297–22299, July 21, 1974.

to the suburbs for tax purposes. This influx of industry brings jobs for the citizens but may deteriorate the quality of life in the community. As we shall see in the next chapter, some communities have adopted noise ordinances to control the noise levels at property lines of the factory site.

Noise from construction equipment produces relatively high outdoor noise levels, as seen in Table 11.1. In addition to typical sound levels in dBA at 50 ft (15.2 m), the corresponding estimated total sound energy in kilowatt-hours per day is shown for each major type of construction equipment. Clusters of equipment at construction sites can produce a steady roar from early morning to the evening hours, sometimes for relatively long periods of time. The number of people in residential areas subjected to construction site noise at various L_{dn} levels was shown in Table 9.2. We recall that several million people are subjected to L_{dn} levels in excess of 60 dBA. This, coupled with construction noise exposure of passersby in urban areas, places construction noise as a major producer of environmental noise pollution.

11.2 A Criterion for Steady-State Noise Exposure

The Committee on Hearing, Bioacoustics and Biomechanics (CHABA), under the auspices of the National Academy of Sciences-National Research Council has developed a criterion[2,3] for steady-state noise exposure that is based on the equal temporary effect theory mentioned earlier. We recall

TABLE 11.2

To Use this Table, Select the Column Headed by the Number of Times the Noise Occurs Per 8-h Workday, Read Down to the Average A-weighted Sound Level of the Noise, and Locate Directly to the Left in the First Column the Total Duration of Dangerous Noise for Any 24-h Period

Cumulative Exposure	Number of Noise Interval Exposures Per 8-h Workday						
	1	3	7	15	35	75	150 or more
8 h	90						
6 h	91	92	93	94	94	94	94
4 h	93	94	95	96	98	99	100
2 h	96	98	100	103	106	109	112
1 h	99	102	105	109	114	115	
30 min	102	106	110	114	115		
15 min	105	110	115				
8 min	108	115					
4 min	111						

Source. CHABA, "Hazardous Exposure to Intermittent and Steady-State Noise," *J. Acoust. Soc. Am.*, Vol. 39, pp. 451–464, 1966.

that this theory relates the long-term hazard of NIPTS to NITTS experienced by young ears in the same environment. The CHABA criterion states[4] that a noise exposure is considered unsafe if an audiometric test, conducted 2 min after cessation of the exposure, reveals one of the following noise-induced temporary threshold shifts (called a TTS_2).

- Average of 10 dB is exceeded at frequencies up to 1000 Hz.
- 15 dB at 2000 Hz.
- 20 dB at 3000 Hz and above.

For practical situations in industrial plants, CHABA recommends the average noise levels in Table 11.2 as it relates to the cumulative exposure time and the number of noise intervals experienced in an 8-h day. A noise interval exists when the exposure level exceeds 80 dBA. If the level drops below 80 dBA for either (1) more than 5 min, or (2) a length of time equal to 1/5 of the average noise interval, then an interruption of exposure is said to exist. For example, if a worker were exposed to 98 dBA on three separate occasions each day, the total cumulative exposure time at that level should not exceed 2 h each day, as seen in Table 11.2.

Example 11.1
A machine automatically operates for 2.5 min, exposing a worker to 100 dBA. After the 2.5-min operation, it is shut off for 1/2 min, during which time the exposure level equals 70 dBA. This process repeats itself throughout the 8-h workday. What is the allowable daily cumulative exposure that the worker may receive in this situation according to the CHABA criterion?

An interruption of exposure occurs each time the machine is turned off, since the noise drops below 80 dBA for a length of time equal to at least 1/5 the average noise interval duration. The number of these noise interval exposures is 20 per hour or 160 per 8-h day. From Table 11.2 we observe that at 100 dBA for 150 or more intervals, the allowable cumulative exposure equals 4 h.   Answer

11.3 Noise Exposure Rating

An industrial worker is frequently exposed to high noise levels of different amounts during an 8-h workday. To determine the severity of this type of noise exposure, the information contained in Table 11.2 is used to calculate the noise exposure rating, NER, which is defined as

$$\text{NER} = \sum_i \frac{C_i}{T_i} \tag{11.1}$$

in which C_i = total exposure time at a given steady noise level
T_i = total exposure time permitted at the corresponding noise level in Table 11.2

If NER < 1, the noise exposure is considered acceptable. In effect, we are prorating the fraction of the exposure time at each allowable noise level contained in Table 11.2 when we calculate the NER. This type of information allows industrial plant management to rotate employees to different stations in a plant to assure that each worker's daily noise exposure does not exceed an NER greater than unity.

Example 11.2
A plant employee works at three different stations. At station 1, the level is continuous at 91 dBA, exposure time 2 h; at station 2, the level is 92 dBA, exposure time 3 h over three separate intervals; at station 3, the level is 89 dBA, exposure time 2.5h over seven separate intervals. Find the noise exposure rating.
    Referring to Table 11.2, we obtain the allowable exposure times for stations 1 and 2.

Station 1: $C_1 = 2\,\text{h}$ $T_1 = 6\,\text{h}$
Station 2: $C_2 = 3\,\text{h}$ $T_2 = 6\,\text{h}$

Station 3 is not included in the calculations, since the level is less than 90 dBA. Substituting into Equation 11.1,

$$\text{NER} = \frac{C_1}{T_1} + \frac{C_2}{T_2}$$
$$= \frac{2}{6} + \frac{3}{6} = \frac{5}{6} \quad \text{Answer}$$

Since the noise exposure rating is less than unity, the exposure of the employee is considered acceptable based on the NER criteria defined in this section.

11.4 Federal Occupational Noise Levels

The Walsh-Healey Public Contracts Act of 1938 was amended in 1969 to include for the first time a federal safety regulation on industrial noise exposure. This meant that companies doing at least $10,000 annual business with the federal government were subjected to the law. At that time approximately 27 million workers were covered by the amended law. Table 11.3 shows the permissible noise exposures adopted by the Walsh-Healey Public Contracts Act. We observe that as the allowable time of exposure is halved, the allowable noise level increases by 5 dBA. This corresponds to seven intervals per 8-h day in Table 11.2, a situation that was assumed for the average working condition (coffee breaks, lunch break, etc.). These same occupational noise levels were included under OSHA in 1970 for industries engaged in interstate commerce.

To account for those employees exposed to two or more periods of noise exposure at different levels, the daily noise dose, D, is calculated as follows.

$$D = \sum_i \frac{C_i}{T_i} \tag{11.2}$$

This equation is identical to the noise exposure rating with the exception that T_i is found from Table 11.3.

Revisions to the 1970 OSHA Act were proposed in 1975. Figure 11.1 shows the permitted noise exposure duration versus the steady-state noise level, in dBA, ranging from 85 dBA to a maximum allowable level of 115 dBA.

TABLE 11.3
Permissible Noise Exposures Under the Walsh-Healey Public Contracts Act, 1969

Duration Per Day (h)	Noise Level dBA Slow Response
8	90
6	92
4	95
3	97
2	100
1.5	102
1	105
1/2	110
1/4 or less	115 max

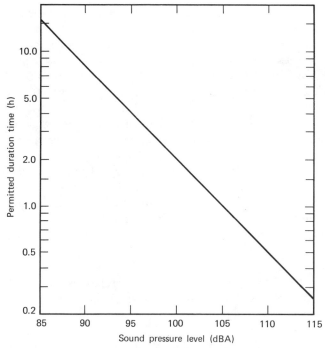

FIGURE 11.1 *Permitted time duration as function of the sound pressure level in accord with the proposed 1975 OSHA requirements.*

This curve is expressed mathematically as

$$T = \frac{16}{2^{(L-85)/5}} \tag{11.3}$$

in which L is the steady-state noise level in dBA, and T is the permitted duration time in hours. Again, we note that as the allowable time of exposure is halved, the allowable level increases by 5 dBA. Under the revisions proposed in 1975, the daily noise dose is calculated using Equation 11.2 with the exception that T_i is obtained from Figure 11.1 or Equation 11.3.

The OSHA regulations define impulse or impact noise as "a sound with a rise time of not more than 35 milliseconds to peak intensity and a duration of not more than 500 milliseconds." Employees shall not be exposed to impulse or impact noise, which exceed 140-dB peak pressure level. Measurements for impulse or impact noise must be made with a Type 1 or Type 2 sound level meter with impulse measurement capability or accessory.

If noise exposures exceed these limits, employees are to wear hearing protective equipment issued by the employer. Furthermore, yearly audiograms are required for these employees as well as for the employees whose daily noise dose equals or exceeds 0.5. Personal protective equipment must also be issued to employees who receive a daily noise dose between 0.5 and 1.0 if their audiograms show any significant decline in hearing level.

There is a significant difference between the recommended noise exposure levels of OSHA and those of EPA, which were discussed in earlier chapters. For example, EPA recommends that an $L_{eq(8)}$ of 75 dBA be applied to industrial situations provided the exposure over the remaining 16 h per day is no greater than an L_{eq} of 60 dBA. This 75 dBA level compares with 90 dBA recommended by OSHA. Likewise, the OSHA regulations allow an increase of 5 dB for each halving of exposure time, while EPA recommends a 3-dB time-intensity tradeoff.[5] Further differences exist for impulse noise, as noted in our earlier treatment of this subject in Chapter 8. The reasons for these significant differences rest primarily on convictions as to whether there is sufficient empirical data and information on the health risk, technological feasibility to control difficult noise situations, and the economic impact of lowering the OSHA levels.

Example 11.3

Rework Example 11.2 for the proposed OSHA regulations of 1975.

The data are arranged in tabular form in which the allowable exposure times are obtained from Equation 11.3.

Station i	Noise Level (dBA)	Exposure Time C_i (h)	Allowable Exposure Time, T_i (h)
1	91	2	6.96
2	92	3	6.06
3	89	2.5	9.19

Using Equation 11.2,

$$D = \frac{2}{6.96} + \frac{3}{6.06} + \frac{2.5}{9.19} = 1.05 \quad \text{Answer}$$

Since the daily noise dose exceeds unity, the proposed OSHA regulations are violated. This means that the employer must first attempt to reduce the noise levels. If this effort fails, the worker's station assignments might be changed to reduce his daily noise dose. If this is not possible, the worker must be issued ear protection equipment and receive yearly audiograms.

11.5 Ear Protection Equipment

The OSHA regulations require that all ear protection equipment be evaluated in accordance with the American National Standard Method for the Measurement of the Real-Ear Attenuation of Ear Protectors at Threshold,

FIGURE 11.2   Examples of molded earplugs.

ANSI Z24.22 (1957). This measurement procedure provides the pure tone attenuation and the corresponding standard deviation as a function of frequency for the ear protection equipment. Having this information, we can calculate the dBA reduction provided by the ear protection equipment in a given noise environment. The noise environment should be known in octave band levels ranging in the center frequencies from 125 to 8000 Hz. Also, we measure or calculate the overall dBA level for the environment. The attenuation of the ear protection equipment should be known at the following frequencies: 125, 250, 500, 1000, 2000, 3000, 4000, 6000, and 8000. The average attenuation is calculated at 3000 and 4000 Hz, and at 6000 and 8000 Hz. Each of the seven attenuations includes a minus correction of 2 standard deviations so that the calculations are applicable to 97.5 percent of the exposed population. These attenuations are subtracted from the octave band levels that have been corrected for A-weighting. The results are added logarithmically to obtain the overall dBA attenuation following the procedures in Chapter 3.

There is a variety of ear protection equipment available to account for individual ear canal configurations.[6] Figure 11.2 shows the size-molded earplugs, which are made of soft flexible material so as to conform to the many different ear canal shapes. To be effective, these earplugs should be snug, airtight, and provide a comfortable fit. Figure 11.3 shows examples of malleable earplugs, which are made of materials such as wax, paper, glass

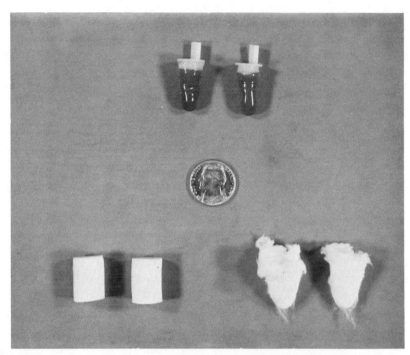

FIGURE 11.3   Examples of malleable earplugs.

FIGURE 11.4   Muff-type ear protectors. (Source. J. Sataloff and P. L. Michael, Hearing Conservation, Charles C. Thomas, p 300, 1973.)

wool, cotton, and mixtures of these and other materials. Usually, the material is worked into the shape of a cone and inserted into the ear canal under sufficient pressure to provide an airtight seal. Figure 11.4 shows an example of muff-type ear protectors. The principal advantages of the muff-type ear protector are that the protection provided is generally greater and less variable between wearers than that of good earplugs. Also, a single size earmuff fits a large percentage of heads. However, they can be uncomfortable in hot weather and are not as compatible with personally worn items like eye glasses as earplugs are.

The type of ear protection equipment will frequently rest with the wearer's preference. However, they should be properly fitted by a physician to assure maximum performance.

Example 11.4

Calculate the noise reduction, R, provided by a set of ear protectors with the following attenuation data, which include the 2 standard deviation corrections at each frequency: 19 dB at 125 Hz, 27 dB at 250 Hz, 37 dB at 500 Hz, 40 dB at 1000 Hz, 40 dB at 2000 Hz, 30 dB for the average of 3000 and 4000 Hz, and 30 dB for the average of 6000 and 8000 Hz. The noise environment is described by the following octave band decibel levels starting at 125 Hz: 91, 89, 92, 92, 92, 88, and 80 dB.

The solution is arranged in tabular form.

i	Octave Band Level	A-weighting Correction	Corrected Octave Band Level, L_i	Attenuation Q_i	$\Delta L_i = L_i - Q_i$
1	91	− 16.1	74.9	19	55.9
2	89	− 8.6	80.4	27	53.4
3	92	− 3.2	88.8	37	51.8
4	92	0	92.0	40	52.0
5	92	+ 1.2	93.2	40	53.2
6	88	+ 1.0	89.0	30	59.0
7	80	− 1.1	78.9	30	48.9

To obtain the overall dBA level of the environment, L_A, add each term logarithmically in column 4, or in the energy summation form,

$$L_A = 10 \log \sum_i 10^{L_i/10} = 97.4 \text{ dBA}$$

The overall attenuated sound, S_A, that reaches the ear is obtained by adding column 6 logarithmically, so that

$$S_A = 10 \log \sum_i 10^{\Delta L_i/10} = 63.0 \text{ dBA}$$

The noise reduction R provided by the ear protectors is

$$R = L_A - S_A = 97.4 - 63.0 = 34.4 \text{ dBA} \qquad \text{Answer}$$

11.6 **Measuring for Industrial Noise**

The requirements for measuring impulse or impact noise under the OSHA regulations are described in Section 11.4. Aside from measuring this special type of noise, OSHA requires that all other noise measurements be made with a sound level meter conforming as a minimum to the requirement of the American National Standard Specification for Sound Level Meters, S 1.4 (1971) Type 2. The meter is set for slow response, A-weighted.

Many OSHA approved audiodosimeters have been developed by manufacturers as a convenient means of checking an employee's daily noise dose. The dosimeter shown in Figure 11.5 can be worn easily by the employee during the daily chores on the job. At the end of the day, the accumulated noise dose is read directly from a digital display that indicates whether this dose is in compliance with the OSHA regulations.

Environmental noise classifiers are useful for monitoring fluctuating noise levels from plant operations, both indoors and outdoors. This instrument, shown in Figure 11.6, provides a histogram over two or three dBA increments. This information can be used to establish the daily noise dose

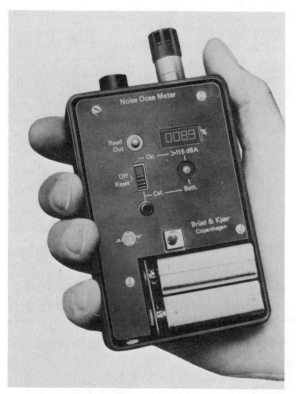

FIGURE 11.5   Personal noise dosimeter. (Courtesy of B & K Instruments, Inc.)

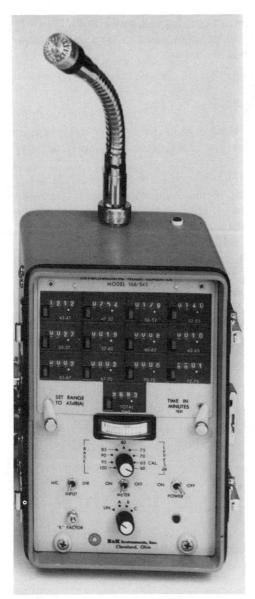

FIGURE 11.6   Environmental noise classifier. (Courtesy of B & K Instruments, Inc.)

for the location where the measurements were made. In outdoor situations, the L_{eq} can be calculated from the noise classifier data as a measure of the impact of the plant noise on the community.

11.7 **Summary**

A. The important ideas:
1. Hearing protection criteria exist for steady-state noise exposure that recommend noise levels, accumulated time, and number of noise intervals for daily exposures over many years.
2. The federal regulations on industrial noise levels include a daily noise dose evaluation for steady-state or interrupted steady-state noise levels with a limit of 115 dBA for unprotected ears.
3. The noise reduction offered by ear protection equipment is calculated with the noise attenuation data provided by the manufacturer.
4. There are many kinds of ear protection equipment designed for a variety of budgets and ear protection requirements.
5. OSHA requires that impulse or impact noise should not exceed 140-dB peak pressure level.
6. Audiodosimeters for personal use are available for evaluating OSHA compliance for fluctuating noise levels.

B. The important equations:

1. $$\text{NER} = \sum_i \frac{C_i}{T_i} \tag{11.1}$$

2. $$D = \sum_i \frac{C_i}{T_i} \tag{11.2}$$

3. $$T = \frac{16}{2^{(L-85)/5}} \tag{11.3}$$

11.8 **Assignments**

11.1 Discuss the problems associated with construction noise.
11.2 Explain what a TTS_2 is and how it is used in evaluating unsafe noise exposure as prescribed by CHABA.
11.3 In the CHABA criterion for steady-state noise, what constitutes an interruption in the noise level exposure?
Find the noise exposure rating for problems 11.4 to 11.7.
11.4 90 dBA, 4 h, continuous,
       92 dBA, 2 h, three noise interval exposures.
11.5 95 dBA, 1 h, seven noise interval exposures,
       94, dBA, 1 h, 35 noise interval exposures.
11.6 102 dBA, 15 min, continuous,
       90 dBA, 5 h, continuous.

11.7 96 dBA, 3 h, continuous,
87 dBA, 5 h, continuous.

11.8 Two machines operate at separate times in a room. Machine A provides 93 dBA for 2 h of continuous operation. How long can machine B be operated within the CHABA guidelines, if it provides 102 dBA for continuous operation?

11.9 Find the daily noise dose for problem 11.4.

11.10 Find the daily noise dose for problem 11.5.

11.11 Find the daily noise dose for problem 11.6.

11.12 Find the daily noise dose for problem 11.7.

11.13 Each morning an employee works in a room for 4 h and is exposed to 90 dBA. How long may this employee work in another room in the afternoon if exposed to 94 dBA? Use the OSHA criteria.

11.14 Discuss the differences between the EPA recommendation on impulse noise and the OSHA regulation on impulse noise.

In the following problems calculate the attenuated sound S_A and the noise reduction R for the ear protection equipment whose sound attenuation is listed in the prescribed order. The octave band levels of the environment, beginning at 125 Hz, follow in each case.

11.15 Attenuation: 13, 20, 30, 33, 42, 41, 28
Environment: 76, 72, 75, 79, 90, 85, 77

11.16 Attenuation: 16, 27, 37, 39, 40, 40, 33
Environment: 91, 87, 87, 88, 86, 80, 76

11.17 Attenuation: 12, 22, 29, 38, 43, 46, 37
Environment: 78, 80, 81, 88, 85, 85, 79

11.18 Attenuation: 27, 36, 41, 39, 47, 48, 40
Environment: 101, 98, 92, 85, 85, 83, 75

11.19 Describe the different types of ear protection equipment. List the advantages and disadvantages of each type.

References

[1] "Noise from Industrial Plants," NTID 300.2, U.S. Environmental Protection Agency, December 1971.

[2] CHABA, "Hazardous Exposure to Intermittent and Steady-State Noise," *J. Acoust. Soc. Am.*, Vol. 39, pp. 451–464, 1966.

[3] L. L. Beranek, *Noise and Vibration Control*, Chapter 17, McGraw-Hill, 1971.

[4] "Information on Levels of Environmental Noise Requisite to Protect Public Health and Welfare with an Adequate Margin of Safety," U.S. Environmental Protection Agency, March 1974.

[5] *Federal Register*, Vol. 39, No. 244, pp. 43802–43809, December 18, 1974.

[6] J. Sataloff and P. Michael, *Hearing Conservation*, Charles C Thomas, 1973.

12
NOISE CONTROL LAWS AND ORDINANCES

Since the days of the early Romans, when chariot racing at night was prohibited, man has managed from time to time to introduce regulations to control community noise. This response to the old adage "there ought to be a law against it" was slow in the evolution of community noise laws. However, with the development of our modern industrial machines, many citizens have voiced their objections to the rising environmental noise pollution encroaching on their lives.

Many of the laws currently in existence[1,2] are called nuisance laws and were developed primarily to restrict unpleasant or annoying sounds that are not easily measured or are difficult to control. These laws are useful in controlling boisterous parties, unnecessary automobile horn blowing, animal noises, and the like. Typical wording in nuisance type ordinances include "unreasonably loud, disturbing, unusual . . . unnecessary noise as to be detrimental to the life or health of any individual or cause discomfort or annoyance to a reasonable person of normal sensitivity." These subjective criteria are difficult to enforce, since one must decide on what is unreasonable, what is unnecessary, and who is a person of normal sensitivity! Interpretations in the courts further weaken the original intent of this type of law.

In recent years, performance standards in zoning codes,[3] which specify maximum allowable noise limits at fixed points, have been introduced to strengthen noise ordinances. Also, some laws now place allowable noise emission levels on transportation vehicles, construction equipment, and other major sources of noise in the community.

12.1 Review of Federal Laws

The National Environmental Policy Act of 1969 has required, since January 1, 1970, that federal agencies consider noise as an influence on the quality of the environment. This has been implemented in the form of environmental impact statements required on all federal actions significantly affecting the human environment.

The Noise Pollution and Abatement Act of 1970 provided a central focus within the Environmental Protection Agency (EPA) for overall environmental noise abatement at the federal level. This Act required that EPA carry on research and studies into environmental noise pollution.

The general policy for federal noise abatement and control rests with the Noise Control Act of 1972. It gives the Administrator of EPA broad responsibilities to protect the public health and welfare from hazardous noise. Some significant parts of the Act include: the promulgation of regulations to limit noise from the operations of interstate motor carriers and railroads; study airport/aircraft operations and make recommendations to the Federal Aviation Administration (FAA) to reduce noise levels from aircraft; publish noise effects on the public health and welfare; promulgate regulations limiting noise emission of products sold within the United States; promulgate labeling regulations; coordinate all federal noise research and control programs; and conduct research and provide technical assistance to state and local governments and disseminate public information on noise.

Under the Department of Transportation (DOT) Act of 1966, the Secretary of DOT is directed to "promote and undertake research and development relating to transportation, including noise abatement, with particular attention to aircraft noise." In November 1969, the FAA published the Federal Aviation Regulation (FAR) Part 36—Noise Standards: Aircraft Type Certification. This rule defines noise limits that certain subsonic jet aircraft must meet at prescribed locations relative to the airport runway during takeoff and landing operations. Additional restrictions are imposed to insure that the aircraft become progressively quieter at flight positions further from the airport.

In April 1972 the Federal Highway Administration (FHWA) issued the Policy and Procedure Memorandum (PPM) 90-2, which sets standards for highway noise levels compatible with different land uses. Some details of these standards were presented in Chapter 9.

The Occupational Safety and Health Act of 1970, already discussed in Chapter 11, mandated the Secretary of Labor to promulgate noise levels that will protect employees of all companies engaged in interstate commerce. These standards have been adopted by the Atomic Energy Commission in its programs and by the Department of Interior for its licensed underground coal mines. The Bureau of Motor Carrier Safety of DOT has extrapolated the OSHA regulations for maximum allowable in-cab noise levels for 10-h periods.

The Department of Housing and Urban Development (HUD) published Policy Circular 1390.2 in August 1971; it established acceptable acoustical environments for new site and existing buildings for HUD funding. Further details of the HUD Circular are found in Chapter 9.

We see that the federal government has only recently obtained broad legislative powers to curb environmental noise pollution. Simultaneously, many state and local governments have become active in noise control legislation, as shown throughout this chapter.

12.2 Controlling Aircraft/Airport Noise

The growth of the air transportation industry[4] can be demonstrated by considering the following statistics. In 1950, 17 million passengers were served by domestic commercial air carriers, which produced 8 billion revenue passenger miles. These numbers grew to 190 million passengers and 152 billion revenue passenger miles by 1972. This phenomenal growth occurred during the introduction of the commercial jet aircraft in the late 1950s, expansion of existing airports to accomodate increased air traffic and larger aircraft, and the development of new airports, which reached 500 major terminals by 1972. Rising noise levels have accompanied this growth, so that several million people in residential areas are subjected to L_{dn} levels in excess of 60 dBA, as shown in Table 9.4.

In 1973 EPA published "Report on Aircraft-Airport Noise" for the Congress as required by the Noise Control Act of 1972. The report surveys the options available to control the impact of aircraft noise on communities. One approach suggests modifications to the existing air carrier fleet by sound absorption material (SAM) in the engine nacelle and bypass duct. Studies indicate that for the Boeing 707 and DC-8 aircraft powered by the JT3D jet engine, which is currently the worst noise offender, the reductions from the SAM treatment would be significant, both for the takeoff and approach modes. Another recommendation from the EPA report is directed at the existing JT3D and JT8D jet engines to include fan modifications and changes in the airflow bypass ratio. These retrofit programs could be effective at reducing aircraft noise, since they are aimed directly at the source.

To curtail the noise from jet aircraft experienced by communities that lie under the flight paths around airports, the EPA study recommends modifications of flight procedures. Some of these noise abatement flight procedures include higher approach glide slopes, two segment approaches, and reduced power thrusts on takeoffs. Needless to say, the air pilots' spokesmen argue that such procedures might endanger the safety of the aircraft.

The FAR 36 Noise Standards have been developed by FAA for certification of subsonic transport and turbojet-powered aircraft. The noise limits of this regulation are expressed in EPNL values, which are related to the gross takeoff weight of the aircraft. Measurements are made at predetermined sites for landing, sideline, and takeoff, as shown in Figure 12.1. For landing and sideline sites, the levels range from 102 to 108 EPNdB, while for takeoff they range from 93 to 108 EPNdB. The certification procedure of new jet aircraft should make a beneficial contribution to reducing individual jet aircraft noise in the long run.

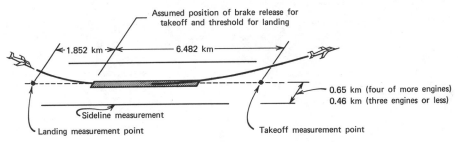

FIGURE 12.1 *Measurement site locations for landing, sideline, and takeoff as prescribed by FAR-36 Noise Standards.*

To date most communities have not included aircraft noise control in their noise ordinances because of the preemptive federal powers of the FAA. However, California has established noise level limits at property boundary lines around airports in terms of the community equivalent noise level (CNEL). A long range goal of 65 dBA after January 1, 1981 has been established for new airports as well as existing airports, regardless of size.

12.3 Controlling Stationary Noise Sources

Some of the newer state and local noise ordinances limit noise levels at property lines and at lines dividing zoning districts in terms of octave band sound pressure levels. The actual numbers selected[5] have been related to the noise criteria (NC) curves, which were a forerunner of the PNC curves in Chapter 7. Nighttime (10 P.M. to 7 A.M.) limits in our cities range from NC-35 to NC-50 with the median at NC-43. Usually 5 dB is added for daytime exposure, although some may add as much as 10 dB.

Instead of using maximum allowable octave band levels at the property lines, some ordinances provide only dBA levels. For example, the Baltimore ordinance, which became effective July 1, 1973, includes such a provision for noise sources located within industrial zones, commercial zones, and res-

TABLE 12.1

No Person Shall Cause, Suffer, Allow or Permit Sound from any Industrial or Commercial Operation that, when Measured at any Residential Property Line, is in Excess of the Following: Continuous Airborne Sound that has an Octave Band Sound Pressure Level in Decibels that Exceeds the Values Listed Below in One or More Octave Bands.

Octave Band Center Frequency (Hz)	Octave Band Sound Pressure Level (dB)		Effective 1/1/76
	Effective 1/18/74		
	7:00 A.M.–10:00 P.M.	10:00 P.M.–7:00 A.M.	10:00 P.M.–7:00 A.M.
31.5	96	89	86
63	82	75	71
125	74	65	61
250	67	58	53
500	63	53	48
1000	60	50	45
2000	57	47	42
4000	55	45	40
8000	53	43	38
Overall dBA	65	55	50

idential zones. The levels vary for each zone and may be exceeded during the daytime as follows: 5 dBA for a duration not to exceed 12 min in any 1 h; 10 dBA for a duration not to exceed 3 min in any 1 h; 15 dBA for a duration not to exceed 30 s in any 1 h. Furthermore, the maximum permissible levels are to be reduced by 5 dBA for sounds of periodic character, impulsive character, or steady audible tones such as a hum, whine, or screech.

Effective January 18, 1974 the state of New Jersey passed a law restricting continuous airborne noise levels at residential property lines in terms of both dBA levels and octave band levels for the daytime and the nighttime. Some of the details of this law are shown in Table 12.1. In addition, this law limits impulse sound levels to 80 dB at the property line. There are similar restrictions on industrial and commercial operations with the measurements being made at the property line of any commercial operation. However, there is no distinction in the New Jersey law between daytime and nighttime levels in industrial and commercial zones.

As a final comment on fixed noise levels allowed at property lines, consider Table 12.2.[6] This table summarizes the average property line levels set by over 100 municipal noise ordinances that exist across the country. It is interesting to note that the average residential levels yield an L_{dn} equal to 60.1 dBA, which is well above the recommended EPA level of 55 dBA.

TABLE 12.2
Summary of National Average Property Line Levels Set by
Municipal Noise Ordinances

District	Average Daytime Level (dBA)	Average Nighttime Level (dBA)
Residential	56.8	52.8
Commercial	63.3	59.2
Industrial	67.5	64.2

12.4 Controlling Surface Transportation Noise Sources

In 1967 California adopted the first state program that included comprehensive performance standards for surface transportation vehicles. Some details of this important act are shown in Table 12.3. There are two major features of the act: regulating noise levels from the operation of vehicles and a graduated reduction of noise levels through the sale of new vehicles. The vehicles are classified as motorcycles, heavy vehicles such as diesel-powered trucks, other motor vehicles and combination of towed vehicles, snowmobiles, and off-highway motor vehicles. The California regulations have served as a guide for other states and local governments in drafting noise ordinances to regulate vehicle noise.

EPA[7] has set noise emission standards for motor carriers engaged in interstate commerce. The standards apply to motor carriers whose gross vehicle weight rating or gross combination weight rating exceed 10,000 lb. Some of the important aspects of this federal law are:

1. Standards for Highway Operations.

   86 dBA at 50 ft with speed limits of 35 mi/h or less.

   90 dBA at 50 ft with speed limits of more than 35 mi/h.

2. Standard for Operation under Stationary Test.

   88 dBA at 50 ft from the longitudinal centerline of the vehicle, when its engine is accelerated from idle with wide open throttle to governed speed with the vehicle stationary, transmission in neutral, and clutch engaged.

3. Visual Exhaust System Inspection.

   Vehicle must be free from defects that affect sound reduction; equipped with muffler or other noise dissipative device; not equipped with any cut-out, by-pass, or similar device.

4. Visual Tire Inspection.

   No vehicle shall have a tire or tires having a tread pattern which as originally manufactured, or as newly retreaded, is composed primarily of cavities in the tread which are not vented by grooves to the tire shoulder or circumferentially to each other around the tire.

TABLE 12.3

I. Operation of vehicles at posted speeds	Speed Limit of 35 mi/h or Less	Speed Limit of More Than 35 mi/h
1. Any motor vehicle with a manufacturer's gross vehicle weight (GVW) of 6000 lb or more and any combination of vehicles towed by such vehicle:		
(a) before 1/1/73	88[a]	90
(b) on and after 1/1/73	86	90
2. Any motorcycle other than a motor-driven cycle	82	86
3. Any other motor vehicle and any combination of vehicles towed by such vehicle	76	82

II. No person shall sell or offer for sale a new motor vehicle:

	Manufactured Dates	Allowable Level (dBA)
1. Any motor vehicle with a GVW of 6000 lb or more	After 1967, before 1973	88
	After 1972, before 1975	86
	After 1974, before 1978	83
	After 1977, before 1988	80
	After 1987	70
2. Any motorcycle	Before 1970	92
3. Any motorcycle, other than a motor-driven cycle	After 1969, before 1973	88
	After 1972, before 1975	86
	After 1974, before 1978	80
	After 1977, before 1988	75
	After 1987	70
4. Any other motor vehicle	After 1967, before 1973	86
	After 1972, before 1975	84
	After 1974, before 1978	80
	After 1977, before 1988	75
	After 1987	70
5. Any snowmobile	After 1972	82
6. New off-highway motor vehicles subject to identification:	On or after 1/1/72, before 1/1/73	92
	On or after 1/1/73, before 1/1/75	88
	On or after 1/1/75	86

[a] All levels are in dBA measured at a distance of 50 ft from the centerline of the roadway.

The City of Chicago, having one of the most comprehensive noise ordinances for a city, has limited noise levels from powered boats 50 ft from shore as follows: before January 1, 1975, 85 dBA and after January 1, 1975, 76 dBA. New York City recently adopted a noise ordinance that specifies among other things that refuse compacting vehicles manufactured or purchased after December 31, 1974 shall not exceed 70 dBA at 10 ft.

12.5 Controlling Construction Noise

In compliance with the Noise Control Act of 1972, EPA is establishing noise emission standards for newly manufactured construction equipment. The portable air compressor, which supplies air for equipment such as rock drills and pavement breakers, was selected[8] as the first candidate toward reducing noise at construction sites. The regulation limits the noise from this equipment to an average sound level of 76 dBA measured at a distance of 7 m (approximately 23 ft). The regulation is effective on January 1, 1978 for new air compressors with rated capacities of 75 to 250 ft^3/min, inclusive, and effective July 1, 1978 for new units with rated capacities above 250 ft^3/min.

At the time the noise regulation was issued, a 76-dBA level represented an average noise reduction of 12 dBA from the noise levels of existing units. It was anticipated that the average increase in sales price of portable air compressors complying with the regulation would not exceed 11 percent for the small units (75 to 250 ft^3/min) or 13 percent for the large capacity units (over 250 ft^3/min).

Table 11.1 lists other construction equipment distributed in commerce that may be regulated by the federal government in this manner.

At present, there are only a few municipal governments that have adopted a comprehensive set of standard performance noise regulations for construction equipment. The regulations include the sale and lease of new construction and industrial equipment, agricultural tractors and equipment, and powered commercial equipment intended for use in residential areas. Some cities identify specific equipment for regulation. For example, New York City regulates noise levels from air compressors, paving breakers, and emergency signal devices.

Some local noise ordinances take a practical approach by restricting the time of day when certain construction equipment may be used. For example, the Chicago ordinance of 1971 includes the following.

> *It shall be unlawful for any person to use any pile driver, shovel, hammer, derrick, hoist tractor, roller or other mechanical apparatus operated by fuel or electric power in building or construction operations between the hours of 9:30 p.m. and 8:00 a.m. except for work on public improvements and work of public service utilities, within 600 feet of any building used for residential or hospital purposes.*

12.6 Measurement Procedures in Ordinances

Provision should be made in a noise ordinance for the procedures to be followed in measuring the noise levels that are subject to the law. Some ordinances temporarily avoid this issue by authorizing the chief administrative officer with the responsibility of developing the methodology for measurements at a later date. Other ordinances refer to recommended measurement procedures adopted by professional societies. For example, most state laws designed to control the noise emitted by snowmobiles require that all measurements shall conform to the Society of Automotive Engineers (SAE) Recommended Practice J 192-"Exterior Sound Levels for Snowmobiles." Similar SAE-recommended practices are frequently found for measuring the noise from automobiles, trucks, and the like. These existing recommended practices have the advantage of being accepted by many professionals and, therefore, will normally hold up in court.

Many ordinances specify that noise measurements must be obtained using a Type 2 or better sound level meter as prescribed by the American National Standard Specifications for Sound Level Meters, ANSI S 1.4-1971. Other provisions may limit outdoor measurements if the wind velocity exceeds a prescribed limit, that a wind screen be always used when measuring outdoor noise levels, and that care be exercised to avoid sound-reflecting surfaces. The instrumentation should be calibrated on a regular basis and be kept in good working order.

12.7 Nuisance Laws

Although modern noise ordinances tend to include decibel limits for noise sources in the community, it may be desirable to incorporate general nuisance regulations as well. Such wording provides a catchall for unforeseen difficulties that may arise. The following recommended language is taken from the NIMLO model ordinance.[1]

> It shall be unlawful for any person to make, continue, or cause to be made or continued any excessive, unnecessary or unusually loud noise or any noise which either annoys, disturbs, injures or endangers the comfort, repose, health, peace or safety of others, within the limits of the city.

The model ordinance goes on to describe certain acts that are declared to be loud, disturbing, and unnecessary noises in violation of the ordinance. Examples of these include horns, operating radios and phonographs under certain conditions, loud speakers, yelling or shouting at certain times of the day, and the shouting of hawkers or peddlers. Barking dogs is one of the most common noise problems in residential communities. The model ordinance addresses this problem by including the following statement as a violation of the law: "The keeping of any animal or bird which by causing frequent or long continued noise shall disturb the comfort or repose of any persons in the vicinity."

12.8 Enforcement and Penalty Features

Most ordinances have specific provisions for the enforcement of the law. In some cases the local police department is used to issue citations to alleged violators, while other jurisdictions have a staff of inspectors from a department concerned with the public health and environmental matters to see that the ordinance is upheld. Another variation includes an enforcement team of one technician who monitors the measurement instrumentation for highway noise violations and one police officer who issues the citation. Some jurisdictions allow the offender a period of time to rectify the noise source, such as a defective muffler in an automobile, with no further penalty on proof of conformance. This approach is likely to win the cooperation of the community with the goals of the noise ordinance.

Convicted violators may be charged with an offense with a maximum fine and/or a period of imprisonment. The following is taken from the Baltimore ordinance as a typical sample found in ordinances that include penalties.

> *Any person, firm, corporation or organization who violates any provision of this ordinance shall be guilty of a misdemeanor, and subject on account thereof to a fine not in excess of ($500.00). Each day of violation shall constitute a separate offense, provided, however, for the purposes of this section, no violation shall be found to have occurred prior to the date of the service of written notice upon the alleged violator as provided in section 282(A).*

12.9 Summary

A. The important ideas:
  1. The federal government has recently taken an active role in environmental noise pollution, particularly with the passage of the Noise Control Act of 1972.
  2. Most ordinances adopted by state and local communities in recent years include maximum allowable decibel levels for major noise sources.
  3. The major targets of noise ordinances include stationary noise sources, transportation vehicles, recreation vehicles, and construction equipment.
  4. Aircraft noise is normally not included in local ordinances due to preemptive powers of the federal government.

5. The success of a noise ordinance depends on local citizen support, an active enforcement program, and clear guidelines on measurement methodology.

12.10 Assignments

12.1 What are the main features of the Noise Control Act of 1972?

12.2 Write a review of the FHWA's PPM 90-2 memorandum on standards for highway noise levels.

12.3 What are the important features of the FAA's FAR Part 36 ruling?

12.4 Summarize the significant parts of the HUD Circular Policy 1390.2.

12.5 What are some of the methods available to control existing aircraft noise?

12.6 Discuss the approaches taken by communities to control stationary noise sources.

12.7 Write a review of the Chicago noise ordinance.

12.8 Write a review of a noise ordinance that applies to your neighborhood. This may be a state or local community ordinance.

12.9 How have state and local governments attempted to control ground transportation noise?

12.10 What in your opinion are the major noise sources in your neighborhood that may require some form of regulation?

References

[1] S. F. Lewin, "Law and the Municipal Ecology, Part Two: Noise Pollution," National Institute of Municipal Law Officers, Washington, D.C. 1970.

[2] J. L. Hilderbrand, "Noise Pollution: An Introduction to the Problem and an Outline for Future Legal Research," *Columbia Law Review*, Vol. 70, April 1970.

[3] C. R. Bragdon, *Noise Pollution—The Unique Crisis*, Chapter 7, University of Pennsylvania, 1970.

[4] "Report on Aircraft-Airport Noise," Environmental Protection Agency, 1973.

[5] L. L. Beranek, *Noise and Vibration Control*, Chapter 18, McGraw-Hill, 1971.

[6] "Model Community Noise Control Ordinance," U.S. Environmental Protection Agency, Washington, D.C., September 1975.

[7] "Motor Carriers Engaged in Interstate Commerce," *Federal Register*, Vol. 39, No. 209, pp. 38208–38216, October 1974.

[8] "Noise Emission Standards for Construction Equipment, Portable Air Compressors," *Federal Register*, Vol. 41, No. 9, pp. 2162–2182, January 1976.

A
SUMMARY OF NOISE RATING METHODS

I. Weighted Sound Pressure Level

The overall sound pressure level in dBA, dBB, or dBC is measured by a sound level meter using an A-, B-, or C-weighting network, respectively. The following table lists the weighting relative response assuming a flat, diffuse-field response for the sound level meter and microphone.

Frequency (Hz)	A-weighting Relative Response (dB)	B-weighting Relative Response (dB)	C-weighting Relative Response (dB)
63	−26.2	−9.3	−0.8
125	−16.1	−4.2	−0.2
250	−8.6	−1.3	0
500	−3.2	−0.3	0
1000	0	0	0
2000	+1.2	−0.1	−0.2
4000	+1.0	−0.7	−0.8
8000	−1.1	−2.9	−3.0

II. Loudness

(a) **Loudness Level.** A contour of equal loudness is called a phon, which is the unit of loudness level of a pure tone equal numerically to the intensity level of a 1000-Hz tone judged to be equally loud.

(b) **Apparent Loudness.** The loudness in sones for pure tones that are additive if the pure tones are widely spaced in the frequency spectrum and about equally loud.

(c) **Loudness.** The loudness in sones for sound spectra that are relatively smooth in a diffuse sound field. For 1/1 octave band sound pressure level measurements,

$$S_{eq} = 0.3 \sum_i S_i + 0.7 \, S_{max}$$

in which S_i = loudness index for ith octave band
S_{max} = maximum loudness index

III. Industrial Noise

Noise Exposure Rating. NER $= \sum_i \dfrac{C_i}{T_i}$

in which C_i = total exposure time at a given steady noise level
T_i = total exposure time permitted at the corresponding noise level in Table 11.2.

Daily Noise Dose. $D = \sum_i \dfrac{C_i}{T_i}$

in which C_i = total exposure time at a given steady noise level
T_i = total exposure time permitted by the proposed OSHA regulations shown in Figure 11.1

IV. Aircraft Noise

(a) **Perceived Noise Level, PNL.** The noise level measured for a single aircraft flyover.

1. Calculate the effective noy value N_t

$$N_t = 0.3 \sum_i N_i + 0.7 \, N_{max} \qquad \text{(1/1 octave band data)}$$

$$N_t = 0.15 \sum_i N_i + 0.85 \, N_{max} \qquad \text{(1/3 octave band data)}$$

in which N_i = noy value for ith octave band

N_{max} = maximum noy value

2. Convert N_t value to the equivalent perceived noise level in PNdB.

(b) **Effective Perceived Noise Level, EPNL.** The noise level measured for a single aircraft flyover.

$$\text{EPNL} = \text{PNL}_{max} + 10 \log \left(\frac{\Delta t}{20} \right) + F$$

in which PNL_{max} = maximum perceived noise level during flyover

Δt = 10-dB downtime

F = correction for the presence of discrete frequency components

(c) **Noise Exposure Forecast, NEF.** A cumulative noise measurement of aircraft noise over a 24-h period measured around an airport.

$$NEF = 10 \log \left(\sum_i \sum_j 10^{NEF_{ij}/10} \right)$$

in which $NEF_{ij} = EPNL_{ij} + 10 \log \left[\dfrac{n_D(ij)}{20} + \dfrac{n_N(ij)}{1.2} \right] - 75$

i = class of aircraft

j = flight path

$n_D(ij)$ = number of daytime flights of aircraft i using flight path j

$n_N(ij)$ = number of nighttime flights of aircraft i using flight path j

V. General Community Noise

(a) **Statistical Level.** The sound pressure level that is exceeded a percentage of the time of observation. For example, the L_{10} is the sound pressure level that is exceeded 10 percent of the time of observation.

(b) **Energy Equivalent Sound Level, L_{eq}.** The constant A-weighted sound level that, in a given situation and time period, conveys the same sound energy as the actual time-varying A-weighted sound.

(c) **Day-Night Average Sound Level, L_{dn}.** The energy equivalent sound level during a 24-h period with a 10-dB weighting applied to nighttime sound levels.

ANSWERS
TO EVEN-NUMBERED
PROBLEMS

Chapter 1
1.2 10 kg
1.4 **(a)** 91.5 m
1.6 74,570 W
1.10 **(a)** 2.301
    (b) 1.936
    (c) 3.163
    (d) -0.357
1.12 **(a)** -6.521
    (b) 6.336
1.14 **(a)** 1.0×10^{12}
    (b) 1.028
1.16 **(a)** 4.365×10^{-2}
    (b) 1.778×10^{-1}
1.18 **(a)** 2.570×10^{3}
    (b) 1.778×10^{8}
1.20 25 Hz, 157 rad/s

Chapter 2
2.4 **(a)** 330 m/s
    (b) 344 m/s
    (c) 353 m/s
2.6 138 m

2.8 **(a)** 344 Hz

(b) 1128 Hz

(c) 34.4 Hz

2.10 0.00277 W/m²

2.12 **(a)** 0.442 W/m²

(b) 0.111 W/m²

Chapter 3

3.2 3.16 W

3.4 **(a)** 133.6 dB

(b) 102.6 dB

3.10 115 dB

3.14 78.7 dB

3.16 85.7 dB

3.20 72.1 dB

3.22 157.5, 198.4

Chapter 4

4.18 68.8 dBA

Chapter 5

5.2 1.88 s

5.4 1.25 s

5.10 22.3 dB

5.12 3.04 m

5.14 6.72 Hz

5.16 1.0×10^7 N/m

5.18 **(a)** 30.9 dB

(b) 36.9 dB

5.20 23.5 dB

Chapter 6

6.12 **(a)** 74 phons

(b) 102 phons

6.14 **(a)** 62 phons

(b) 94 phons

(c) 102 phons

(d) 84 phons

6.16 104 phons at 1000 Hz

6.18 **(a)** 66.6 dBA

(b) 15.3 sones, 79 phons at 1000 Hz

Chapter 7
7.6 43.3 dB

7.8 66 dBA

Chapter 8
8.6 143 dB

8.10 no

Chapter 9
9.2 $L_{10} = 85$ dBA

$L_{50} = 72$ dBA

$L_{90} = 60$ dBA

9.6 **(a)** 74.4 dBA

(b) 76.9 dBA

9.8 67.3 dBA

9.10 6 min

9.12 77.0 dBA

9.14 2.8 min

9.16 86.6 dBA

9.20 107.4 dB(NP)

9.22 72.7 dB(NP)

Chapter 10
10.6 112 PNdB

10.10 38.8, (73.8 ± 3) dBA

10.12 Site No. 1—clearly acceptable

Site No. 2—normally unacceptable

10.16 63.5 dBA

10.18 65.5 dBA at 500 ft

59.6 dBA at 1000 ft

Chapter 11
11.4 5/6

11.6 9/8

11.8 15 min

11.10 0.468

11.12 1.27

11.16 $S_A = 60.5$ dBA

$R = 31.7$ dBA

11.18 $S_A = 59.8$ dBA

$R = 34.9$ dBA

INDEX